LET'S WRITE!

CYNTHIA M. STOWE

THE CENTER FOR APPLIED
RESEARCH IN EDUCATION
West Nyack, New York 10994

Library of Congress Cataloging-in-Publication Data

Stowe, Cynthia.
    Let's write! : a ready-to-use activities program for learners with
special needs / Cynthia Stowe.
        p.   cm.
    ISBN 0-87628-521-3 (pbk.)
    1. Learning disabled children—Education (Elementary)—United
States.   2. English language—Composition and exercises—Study and
teaching (Elementary)—United States.   3. Education, Elementary—
Activity programs—United States.   I. Center for Applied Research
in Education.   II. Title.
    LC4704.85.S75   1997
    371.9 0472—dc21   97-25821
                                                                CIP

The border illustrations on the student activity sheets are from *Allover Patterns with
Letter Forms* by Jean Larcher, part of the Dover Pictorial Archives Series, and used with
permission from Dover Publications, Inc.

Printed in the United States of America

10 9 8 7 6 5 4 3 2 1

ISBN 0-87628-521-3 (spiral)

ATTENTION: CORPORATIONS AND SCHOOLS

The Center for Applied Research in Education books are available at
quantity discounts with bulk purchase for educational, business, or sales
promotional use. For information, please write to: Prentice Hall Career &
Personal Development Special Sales, 240 Frisch Court, Paramus, NJ
07652. Please supply: title of book, ISBN number, quantity, how the book
will be used, date needed.

**THE CENTER FOR APPLIED
RESEARCH IN EDUCATION**
West Nyack, NY 10994
A Simon & Schuster Company

On the World Wide Web at http://www.phdirect.com

Prentice Hall International (UK) Limited, *London*
Prentice Hall of Australia Pty. Limited, *Sydney*
Prentice Hall Canada, Inc., *Toronto*
Prentice Hall Hispanoamericana, S.A., *Mexico*
Prentice Hall of India Private Limited, *New Delhi*
Prentice Hall of Japan, Inc., *Tokyo*
Simon & Schuster Asia Pte. Ltd., *Singapore*
Editora Prentice Hall do Brasil, Ltda., *Rio de Janeiro*

This book is dedicated to Cynthia Conway Waring,
dear friend in teaching,
dearest friend in life.

ACKNOWLEDGMENTS

I would also like to acknowledge the following people:

Robert Stowe, who makes everything possible . . .

Susan Kolwicz, for all that she has done for me and for this book, both as an editor and as a friend . . .

The staff and students at Eagle Mountain School, who inspire me and make me laugh . . .

Diana Hanbury King, who, in a workshop many years ago, introduced me to the concepts of writing lists and structured paragraphs with students.

ABOUT THE AUTHOR

Cynthia M. Stowe has taught writing for many years. She is a certified classroom teacher, special education teacher, and school psychologist. She has taught writing to students of all ages, including adults.

Cynthia's main area of interest has always been working with students with special needs. Because she found that these students do not always flourish with traditional writing programs, she developed *Let's Write!* over a twelve-year period while she was working in public school, private school, and clinic settings.

Currently, Cynthia is teaching writing to students with special needs at the Eagle Mountain School in Greenfield, Massachusetts. She has taught many writing workshops to teachers and to parents with their children present.

Cynthia is also an author. She has published three children's books: *Home Sweet Home, Good-Bye* (middle grades, Scholastic, 1990), *Dear Mom, in Ohio for a Year* (middle grades, Scholastic, 1992), and *Not-So-Normal Norman* (grades 3–6, Albert Whitman, 1995). In addition, she has recently published *Spelling Smart! A Ready-to-Use Activities Program for Students With Spelling Difficulties* (The Center for Applied Research in Education, 1996).

ABOUT THIS RESOURCE

Let's Write! is a program designed for students in grade 3 and up who have difficulty with writing. These students often have little confidence in their abilities in this area. They have trouble starting a writing task, and they experience frustration when trying to organize their thoughts on paper. The mechanics of written language present many difficulties. For these students, writing is not a joyful and satisfying task. Rather, it is overwhelming and agonizing.

Why do these students need a special program to help them learn to write? Why can't a good writing program recommended for all students be presented at a slower pace? Why isn't it enough just to provide more support of the writing process for these students?

Students who are reluctant writers show us by their behavior that some of their needs are unique. These students often verbalize easily and well. Many of them have wonderful, creative imaginations and curious minds. They could become fabulous writers. They can, in fact, succeed in this area if attention is given to their special needs.

WHAT ARE THESE SPECIAL NEEDS?

The following are main areas of need.

1. Some students may be hyperactive or have difficulty paying attention. Whether they are labeled ADHD (Attention Deficit Hyperactivity Disorder), or it is just known that they have short attention spans, it is difficult for them to attend independently to a writing task.
2. Some students have visual motor coordination problems. This makes the physical act of writing cumbersome and slow.
3. Some students have visual memory issues. This often leads to frustration with spelling, which can make writing unpleasant. For example, some students will avoid words they are afraid they cannot spell, and this breaks their train of thought for fluent writing. Others are so insecure about spelling that they resist putting any words on paper.
4. Some students have auditory memory issues. This often makes it hard for them to hear and remember the grammatical structure of English, and thus they feel uncomfortable with grammar in their writing. These students often confuse verb tenses, and also make other errors that affect meaning.

5. Some students have difficulty with organization. They have trouble stating the main idea, and their work often contains strings of free associations. Details are not placed in natural sequences.

6. Some students have emotional needs. Whatever the cause, they appear to have low motivation for writing. Some are openly resistive. These students often have habitual patterns of not working at their writing—of not "trying."

HOW CAN THESE SPECIAL NEEDS BE MET?

The following are ways that *Let's Write!* meets these needs.

1. Structures for written language are provided. Whereas these structures do not have to be rigidly adhered to, they help many students become comfortable with sentences, paragraphs, and longer works.

2. The experiential approach is used. Activities and instruction are presented in a way that asks students to be active rather than passive learners. This increases their motivation and gets them more involved with their learning.

3. The sequential presentation of the skills needed for successful writing helps students become successful right from the start of their program.

4. Multimodality instruction is used. This allows students' areas of strength to be tapped for writing.

5. Each lesson consists of four different parts, each of which utilizes different skills. For example, one lesson (of a moderate degree of difficulty) could ask students to do the following:

    a. write a list of things that can fly
    b. write a paragraph about a favorite meal
    c. play a game that involves pantomiming verbs
    d. listen to a read-aloud like *The Education of Little Tree.*

    Instead of staying with one specific task for an extended period of time, students spend smaller amounts of time on diverse tasks, which helps greatly with attention and hyperactivity issues.

6. Interesting and varied opportunities for practice are provided. As with other skills, students get better as they write more.

7. Insistence on a student's ability to be independent throughout the program is crucial. *Let's Write!* is designed so that students can always write for themselves.

HOW IS LET'S WRITE! STRUCTURED?

In the introductory section "How to Use This Program," the philosophy and methodology of *Let's Write!* are presented. Guidelines on how to plan a lesson are included, as well as examples of typical lessons. The different areas of instruction possibilities (such as report writing and poetry) are summarized. Important issues, such as the pacing of lessons, the choice between print and cursive writing, the correction of spelling errors in writing, and the use of word processors, are discussed.

Let's Write! consists of two major parts. Part One focuses on teaching the basic structures of written language. The chapters on Word Writing, Sentence Writing, Paragraph Writing, Research Reports, Book Reports, Stories, and Essays each contain a narrative that gives specific information on that particular area of writing. Then, activities and games are presented. Finally, activity sheets are provided for independent work for all but the Essay chapter.

Part Two offers two different things: specific skill development and opportunities for practice. The following are covered: Grammar, Editing, Poetry, The Literature Connection, Holidays, Writing Letters, Using the Newspaper, Integrating Writing With Real Life and the Rest of the Curriculum, and Gimmicks and Gags. As with Part One, each of these chapters has a narrative that discusses the area. Then, activities and games are presented to help teach the skills needed. Last, activity sheets are provided for independent work.

Two appendixes are provided at the end of this book. Appendix A offers a discussion of list writing and gives favorite ideas for word, phrase, and sentence lists. Appendix B offers a short discussion about reading aloud and gives suggestions for resources in this area.

A typical lesson will consist of:

1. a list (refer to Appendix A)
2. writing that teaches the structures of written language (select from Part One)
3. writing or doing an interactive activity that either teaches a skill or provides practice (select from Part Two)
4. reading aloud (refer to Appendix B).

CONTENTS

About This Resource . . . . *ix*

How to Use This Program . . . . *xix*

PART ONE

WORD WRITING **3**

Grammar Concepts Presented at This Level   5

Editing Concepts Presented at This Level   5

    ACTIVITIES   6

Reproducibles:

    A Category Game (1)   9

    A Category Game (2)   10

    Find the Right Word! (1)   11

    Find the Right Word! (2)   12

    An Interview of a Fellow Student   13

    An Interview of an Adult in the School or Community   14

    Riddles (1)   15

    Riddles (2)   16

    Fill in the Blanks (1)   17

    Fill in the Blanks (2)   18

    ANSWER KEY   19

SENTENCE WRITING **20**

How to Begin the Actual Writing of Sentences   21

Grammar Concepts Presented at This Level   23

Editing Concepts Presented at This Level   23

    ACTIVITIES   24

Reproducibles:

    Write It With Nouns   28

    Write It With Verbs   29

    Write It With Subjects   30

    Write It With Predicates   31

    Write It With Challenge Words   32

    A Description   33

    About Me (1)   34

    About Me (2)   35

An Interview   36

Write It With Questions   37

PARAGRAPH WRITING 38

Reproducibles:

  Figure 1. The Start of a Paragraph   40

  Figure 2. A Paragraph   42

  Figure 3. Paragraphs for Sequencing Skills   43

Grammar Concepts Presented at This Level   45

Editing Concepts Presented at This Level   45

  ACTIVITIES   45

Reproducibles:

  Write About an Animal   51

  A "How-To" Paragraph   52

  An Opinion Paragraph   53

  A "What If" Paragraph   54

  A "Can You Beat This?" Paragraph   55

  A "Find the Lies" Paragraph   56

WRITING RESEARCH REPORTS 57

The Four Levels of Report Writing   58

Two Issues   60

  POSSIBLE WRITING TOPICS   60

Reproducibles:

  Write About an Animal   64

  Report on a Place (1)   65

  Report on a Place (2)   66

  Write About Places   67

  Write About a Person   68

  Write About Amazing Facts   69

  Write About an Object of the Future   70

  Write About an Imaginary Place   71

  Write an Autobiography   72

WRITING BOOK REPORTS 73

Traditional Book Reports   73

  10 BOOK REPORT ACTIVITIES   74

Reproducibles:

  A Book Report (1)   77

  A Book Report (2)   79

A Book Report (3)   *81*

A List   *83*

Write a Testimonial   *84*

Questions for a TV News Interview   *85*

Write a Diary   *86*

WRITING STORIES 87

A Note on Sharing   88

ACTIVITIES   89

Reproducibles:

A Story (1)   *92*

A Story (2)   *93*

A Story (3)   *94*

A Story (4)   *95*

A Story (5)   *96*

A Story (6)   *97*

Story Starters   *98*

Five-Object Find (1)   *101*

Five-Object Find (2)   *102*

Five-Object Find (3)   *103*

Five-Object Find (4)   *104*

A Very Long Excuse—Story Starters   *105*

This Is How I . . . Story Starters   *108*

Help! There's an . . . ABC Story   *110*

WRITING ESSAYS 112

Reproducibles:

"Write About" Topics for Short Essays   *114*

Political Topics for Short Essays   *115*

Personal and Moral Topics for Short Essays   *116*

PART TWO

GRAMMAR 119

Which Grammar Concepts Should Be Taught, and When Should
      They Be Presented?   119

How to Teach Grammar Concepts and Usage   122

ACTIVITIES   122

Reproducibles:

> *Write the Most Nouns Contest Rules*   127
>
> *Where Does the Word Belong?*   128
>
> *Finish These Sentences (1)*   129
>
> *Finish These Sentences (2)*   130
>
> *Search and Destroy*   131
>
> *Can You Read This?*   132

EDITING 133

Specific Techniques for Teaching Self-Editing Skills   135

> Independent Activities   137
>
> Teaching Self-Editing at the Advanced Level   137

Reproducibles:

> *Find My Mistakes (1)*   138
>
> *Find My Mistakes (2)*   139
>
> *Find My Mistakes (3)*   140

WRITING POETRY 141

Reading Poems   141

> ACTIVITIES   143

Reproducibles:

> *A Pizza Poem (Example)*   147
>
> *A Backpacking Trip (Example)*   150
>
> *Never Will I Ever*   153
>
> *An Alphabet Poem*   154
>
> *A City Poem*   156
>
> *A Pattern Poem*   157
>
> *A Tell-It-Like-It-Is Poem*   158
>
> *Rhyming Pairs*   159
>
> *A Poem Full of Lies*   160

THE LITERATURE CONNECTION 161

ACTIVITIES   161

Reproducibles:

> *A Turnip Story*   169
>
> *Don't Lie a Little, Lie a Lot*   170
>
> *More Lies*   171
>
> *Animal Questions*   172
>
> *Good or Bad?*   173

HOLIDAYS 174

Talking About Holidays   175
    HOLIDAY ACTIVITIES   175
Reproducibles:
    What I Found in My Bag After Halloween   180
    A Candle Poem   181
    A Thanksgiving Poem   182
    A Holiday from the Past   183
    A Holiday from Another Culture   184
    If They Met   185

WRITING LETTERS 186

Writing Friendly Letters   186
Writing Business Letters   187
Reproducible:
    Bad Letter and Better Letter (Example)   188
    ACTIVITIES   190
Reproducibles:
    Something New   194
    It's Horrible!   195
    Believe It!   196
    It's Very Strange Here   197
    These Earth People Are Too Much!   198
    Hello Human   199

USING THE NEWSPAPER 200

    ACTIVITIES   201
Reproducibles:
    An Advertisement   205
    Job Wanted   206
    Someone Special   207
    Dear Gertrude   208
    It Really Happened   209
    A Tale Retold   210

INTEGRATING WRITING WITH REAL LIFE AND THE REST OF THE CURRICULUM 211

    ACTIVITIES   211

Reproducibles:

Banking Forms   216

Checks   217

A Job Application   218

GIMMICKS AND GAGS **219**

ACTIVITIES   219

Games That Develop Auditory and Verbal Skills   219

Activities and Games for the Development of
      Word Writing   220

Activities and Games for the Development of
      Sentence Writing   222

Activities for the Development of Paragraph Writing   223

Reproducibles:

A Tin Can Label   225

An Architectural Drawing   226

A Map   227

A Menu   228

Write Directions   229

Draw a Monster   230

A TV Commercial   231

A Ridiculous Interview   232

APPENDIX A

LIST IDEAS **233**

APPENDIX B

READ-ALOUD BOOKS **237**

HOW TO USE THIS PROGRAM

THE PHILOSOPHY AND METHODOLOGY OF LET'S WRITE!

Let's Write! is based on the following beliefs.

1. All students can learn to enjoy writing once they are provided with opportunities where they can be successful.
2. All students can develop their writing skills.
3. The organization of written language is a key element in teaching writing to students with difficulties in this area. Once students see writing as a task that has order and meaning, they are more likely to approach it with confidence.
4. Lessons must be structured and predictable.
5. Teachers should write along with students on all writing assignments. Even though this seems difficult at times, because teachers feel that they should be helping students, it is a vital aspect of the program.

    Writing along with students changes the feeling, "The teacher is making me do this," to "We're working together." Also, when teachers write, they can model good writing skills.
6. Students and teachers should share their work on a regular basis. Supportive feedback is always given. When responding to students' writing, it is best to comment on the content of the work. For example, if a student has written a description of her home in which she has mentioned that there is a rock wall in the living room, you could say, "A rock wall! That's amazing. Did someone you know build it?" This is a more powerful response than a simple, "Great job!" because it lets the student know that she has conveyed interesting information in her writing.
7. All students can learn to become independent writers. At whatever level they function, they can experience the satisfaction of doing the work themselves.

OF WHAT DOES A TYPICAL LESSON CONSIST?

An optimal amount of time for writing instruction is one hour for each session. Within that time, four different activities are presented. It is not necessary to finish one activity before moving on to another. For example, if a student is working on a story, she will work on it for the allotted time of approximately fifteen to twenty minutes. She will then proceed to the next activity and will return to her story only at the next lesson.

If one hour is not available, it is still best to base each lesson plan on that amount of time. Individual activities can be presented sequentially over a span of days, if necessary.

Let's Write! can be used with individuals or for small groups. It can be used for large groups if students have similar functioning levels and needs.

THE FIRST ACTIVITY OF THE LESSON

Every lesson begins with writing a list. This helps with motivation because it's fun and nonthreatening. It also provides essential practice with the generation of ideas. If students are just beginning, they can write such lists as "Things in This Room." If they are very advanced, they can write such lists as "Excuses for Not Doing Homework." A full discussion of list writing and favorite ideas for lists are provided in Appendix A.

THE SECOND ACTIVITY OF THE LESSON

In this section of the lesson, students focus on learning the basic structures of written language. Select an activity from Part One.

Start at the "Word Writing" chapter. If students appear confident and capable at this level, proceed to the "Sentence Writing" chapter. Once students are asking for more challenge, go on to "Paragraph Writing," and so on. You will quickly discover where your students need to spend the most time.

The following gives a sampling of what can be found in each chapter of Part One.

1. **Word Writing.** Students practice writing words and phrases as they complete such activities as creating word collections and making games. These activities make the word writing practice meaningful.

2. **Sentence Writing.** Students practice writing sentences as they express their opinions on a variety of subjects; for example, "What do you think about watching TV? Is it a waste of time, or a good way to learn?" Students are also offered the opportunity to write about themselves and to conduct interviews.

3. **Paragraph Writing.** Structured paragraph writing is taught. Students practice with topic sentences, supporting detail sentences, and ending sentences. They do this frequently, until they are able to leave the rigid form, and can independently and easily write well-organized paragraphs.

4. **Research Reports.** Students work on reports with varying degrees of support. At the earliest levels, art can be an important aspect of report

writing, and you provide the organizational structure of the report. At the most advanced levels, students work independently, doing their own research and developing their information in a logical order.

5. **Book Reports.** Students report on books they have read. These reports can be traditional or nontraditional. An example of the latter is writing a diary of a character, which begins after the published story has finished.

6. **Stories.** Students do some creative writing. Activities can range from writing very long excuses to realistic fiction. A number of stimulus ideas at varying levels of difficulty are presented.

7. **Essays.** Students express their opinions and beliefs about a wide variety of subjects. These can include historical or current events. Possible essay topics are listed at the end of the chapter.

THE THIRD ACTIVITY OF THE LESSON

Once the activity from Part One has been worked on for approximately fifteen to twenty minutes, proceed to the third section of the lesson. To do this, select an activity from Part Two. The activities in this section have different purposes. Some are designed primarily to teach skills, such as editing, or to introduce important information about the grammatical structure of written language. Others provide practice opportunities. Since the best way to become a competent writer is to write, it's important for students to write a lot at the level where they feel comfortable. Other activities and games in Part Two are mostly fun. These are introduced to help students learn to like to write.

As in Part One, each chapter in Part Two has the following:

- a narrative about the area being covered,
- suggested activities and games, and
- independent activity sheets for reinforcement and practice.

The following describes the chapters in Part Two.

1. **Grammar.** Students are introduced to a few key concepts. They learn about the structure of sentences: about subjects (who or what the sentence is about) and predicates (what is happening), so that they can become aware of both incomplete and run-on sentences in their work. By the end of the program, they will have learned about nouns, verbs, adjectives, adverbs, pronouns, conjunctions, prepositions, and articles. They will also have discovered basic rules about punctuation and capitalization.

Grammar is presented in a slow and relaxed manner, with many multimodality and experiential opportunities for learning. Grammar is not offered as an excessively detailed, oppressive body of knowledge, but rather as interesting information that helps written language become organized.

2. **Editing.** Students develop the skills they need to edit their own work. Editing is presented very slowly, with emphasis on the sequential acquisition of skills. In such activities as "Find My Mistakes," you present a small amount of text containing errors easily recognizable to the student. Great emphasis is placed on offering instruction and activities that make students feel confident about self-editing, since they have so often previously experienced feelings of failure around the number of errors in their work.

3. **Poetry.** A wide variety of possibilities is presented, such as writing first-letter game poems and shape poems. The poems can entail word, phrase, or sentence writing.

4. **The Literature Connection.** Students are offered activities that take advantage of the rich variety of the world's literature. Usually, the literature is used as a stimulus for writing. For example, a book that chronicles one or more great events can be read to students. They can then be asked to write a newspaper article that reports on one of the important occurrences. Various multicultural literature is presented, and activities at all levels are offered.

5. **Holidays.** Rather than see holidays as disruptions to the curriculum, *Let's Write!* sees them as opportunities to engage students in enjoyable and meaningful writing. Whether students are making a holiday statement quilt or composing essays about Kwanzaa, they often are highly motivated.

6. **Writing Letters.** Students are offered real opportunities to communicate. They can write postcards and letters to their friends and family, or they can write letters to businesses. They can also be creative. For example, in one activity, they pretend that they are visiting an unknown planet, and they write a letter back home to describe the strange place in which they find themselves.

7. **Using the Newspaper.** Newspapers are rich resources that offer numerous writing opportunities. Not only do newspapers give current and local news about which students can write opinions, they also provide interesting "tidbits," such as scientific information or human interest stories. Often, the photos in newspapers can provide the stimuli for creative writing. In this chapter, students are given the chance to write the actual parts of a newspaper. They can also work on spin-offs

from regular features, such as a "Job Wanted" ad instead of a "Help Wanted" ad.

8. **Integrating Writing With Real Life and the Rest of the Curriculum.** Students often appreciate learning such "real-life" skills as how to write checks and how to fill out job applications. They also enjoy using their writing in such other subject areas as mathematics. Here, they can write word problems for other students to solve. The highly motivating quality of all of this work is appealing.

9. **Gimmicks and Gags.** At times, students will need to relax and to change the focus from the hard work that writing can be. In this section, ideas are offered to help students have fun with writing; for example, one activity involves music. In this, students take a large piece of paper and fold it into four sections. Four types of music are played (e.g., rock, country, classical, and jazz) and students are asked to draw whatever each type of music inspires them to create. Then, they can write about each drawing.

THE FOURTH ACTIVITY OF THE LESSON

For the last part of each lesson, read to the students for approximately ten minutes. This is included in each lesson because to produce written language, one must listen carefully to it. Encourage good listening skills during this read-aloud time by introducing conversations about the piece being read.

Reading aloud to students is also a time where everyone can relax. This encourages the development of positive feelings for writing instruction. A discussion of read-aloud techniques and suggestions for good read-aloud material are presented in Appendix B.

ABOUT WRITING NOTEBOOKS

Give every student a loose-leaf notebook and a set of colored indexes. Students then write on loose-leaf wide-lined paper (not college-lined) and, when they are done, they file each of their papers in their notebooks. They create their own filing system by writing needed categories for their indexes, such as: Paragraphs, Poetry, Grammar, Creative Writing, and so forth. All writing papers should be dated and saved. Students like to see what they have done in the past and the progress they have made.

It can be expensive to buy these notebooks and indexes. Sometimes, they can be bought in bulk at office supply stores; occasionally, they are on sale at discount stores. If possible, obtain these supplies for your students. It helps students feel ownership of their own written work, because they are keeping track of it.

Also, and possibly most critical, keeping and filing their work supports the development of organizational skills.

THREE SAMPLE LESSON PLANS

The following are offered to show how lessons can be planned using this resource.

Lesson One (at a Beginning Level of Difficulty)

FIRST ACTIVITY: Write a list of things that are green.

SECOND ACTIVITY: (from Part One, "Word Writing") Write down good action words like "jump" and "pull," and act out selected ones for peers to guess, as in charades.

THIRD ACTIVITY: (from Part Two, "Gimmicks And Gags") Make a map of the room, and label selected parts of the room and objects in the room.

FOURTH ACTIVITY: Read from *The Red Comb* by Fernando Picó.

Lesson Two (at a Moderate Level of Difficulty)

FIRST ACTIVITY: Write a list of things made out of glass.

SECOND ACTIVITY: (From Part One, "Paragraph Writing") Write a paragraph about computers. A topic sentence can be: Computers are useful tools.

THIRD ACTIVITY: (from Part Two, "Writing Letters"—a creative writing activity) Write a "Hello Human" letter. Pretend that you are an animal who wishes to communicate with a person, and you plan to tell that human exactly what you want her to know.

FOURTH ACTIVITY: Read from *Sing Down the Moon* by Scott O'Dell.

Lesson Three (at an Advanced Level of Difficulty)

FIRST ACTIVITY: Write a list of reasons for not smoking cigarettes.

SECOND ACTIVITY: (from Part One, "Research Reports") Work on a report about the different cultures in Mexico.

THIRD ACTIVITY: (from Part Two, "Poetry") Work on a funny poem that is full of lies.

FOURTH ACTIVITY: Read from *Summer Of My German Soldier* by Bette Greene.

ISSUES AND CONCERNS

1. Where should students begin, and how fast should they proceed through the program?

The two key words to consider as you answer these questions are *comfort* and *challenge.* Beginning writers need them both. They need to feel that they are being asked to do something of which they are capable. For this reason, in every part of the lesson, students must practice below their frustration level. For example, if they can write words fairly easily but find it hard to write sentences, they should be given many opportunities to write words. Sentence writing should be introduced slowly and with a great deal of support.

Students also need to feel that they are progressing; it is important to frequently offer new skills and higher level work. Watch your students carefully at these times. If they begin to act in a negative way, either by withdrawing or by acting out, it is probably best to return to more comfortable levels of writing. Continue to offer more difficult work at various times. When they are ready, your students will be excited by the advancement.

2. Should students print or use cursive?

Legible and fluent cursive writing is a goal for all students. Because the letters are connected within words in cursive, many of the spatial difficulties some students have with printing are eliminated. In other words, it's easier for them to separate words from one another. Also, once students become capable with cursive writing, it is faster and easier for them than using print.

If your students are not able to write in cursive when they begin *Let's Write!* then let them print; however, in a separate part of the day, teach them cursive writing.

3. Should improper spelling be corrected?

The basic answer to this is "No." Often, reluctant writers have corresponding difficulties with spelling. They may have received negative feedback in this area in the past. Even if teachers and parents have corrected their spelling in a nurturing way, students often feel insecure about their skills.

If you focus on spelling in the beginning of writing instruction, it may be a negative reminder of a weakness. With *Let's Write!* you focus on students' strengths: their good thinking skills and natural enjoyment of language.

Teach spelling in a separate part of the curriculum. Once students are competent spellers and fluent writers, you can help them begin to self-edit their work. Specific suggestions on how to help students self-edit are offered in the "Editing" section of this resource.

4. Should students use word processors?

With *Let's Write!* students primarily use pencil and paper for writing. Students must learn how to write in this way both in real-life situations, such as filling out job applications, and for other school subjects, such as when they're asked to answer essay questions on tests. They need to practice forming thoughts into hand-written language.

Also, it is more convenient to hand-write in many situations. Even though computers are becoming more widely available, we don't often carry them on long walks, to rest under a tree and write a poem, or sit in a coffee shop and work on a story.

Word processors are, however, powerful and useful writing tools. Once students are capable writers, they should learn keyboarding skills. An excellent program is *Keyboarding Skills* by Diana Hanbury King (Educators Publishing Service, Inc., 1988). This sequential program uses the alphabet as the basic structure for learning to type.

If a student is an extremely reluctant hand-writer because of visual motor issues, but is capable on the keyboard, allow him to complete some of his writing on the computer. Your discretion and wisdom are the best guide.

PART ONE

Word Writing   3

Sentence Writing 20

Paragraph Writing 38

Writing Research Reports . . . 57

Writing Book Reports 73

Writing Stories 87

Writing Essays 112

WORD WRITING

The ability to write individual words is the basis of all writing. For some students, this is a challenge. These students may not yet understand the connection of letters to sounds and, therefore, all written language is confusing to them. It is important for these students to receive instruction in sound-symbol correspondence as soon as they begin their writing work. It is not critical that they are fully aware of this connection before they begin to write, but they do need an awareness that sounds are attached to letters in a meaningful way. For these students, their writing work can support the work they are doing with sound-symbol correspondence.

For very beginning students, offer models of written words if students are unable to use, or are uncomfortable with, spelling on their own. Models should be clearly written with legible print on the same type of lined paper the students are using. Often, spaces between models help students copy with ease. If multiple word models are being used, ask students to cross out those that have already been copied.

As you present these models, if you know that students have been learning a particular sound-symbol correspondence, you can point out this relevant element. At the earliest stage, it is especially helpful to point out initial consonant sounds.

Providing word models does not inhibit students from trying to spell once they feel capable of doing so. Invariably, students will naturally begin to try to write their own words when they are ready. They often do not say anything about this, but rather just start writing. It's best to accept these new efforts without much verbal notice, as though something very natural has just occurred. It has! Too much notice at this stage sometimes inhibits students from continuing their new independent writing.

As with providing written models for students who are asked to write, you must also provide as much support as is needed with reading any text that is a part of the lesson. Try to include only words that students can read independently. If this is not possible, however, students can relax knowing that you will help them read any text if they feel confused or overwhelmed.

At this early stage, it is important to ask yourself whether any of your students have verbal issues. Can they think of words to say? Are the needed words in their memory banks, but they have difficulty expressing them? If a student has serious difficulties in either of these areas, request a speech and language evaluation. Once this is done, a speech therapist can assist your work with this student.

If students have difficulties with word retrieval, or expressive language or other language issues, they still can begin work in writing. This will, indeed, support the work they are doing in the speech area. It is important, however, for students to be successful in every lesson.

At the most basic level, concrete objects are provided. For example, if students are writing down things that are red, place several objects that are red on the table. Then, model the words for the students. Say, "I am going to write down the word 'ball' because that ball on the table is red." Say the word and then write it.

This activity can be repeated countless times with variations on the theme of the objects on the table. Students don't seem to tire of it. As long as there are new objects, they think it is fun. It is very rewarding when students begin to add their own ideas of things that belong to whatever category is being presented.

Pictures can be used to stimulate language, as well as objects. Begin with objects for students with serious verbal issues, however. The basic principles are:

1. Present lessons that are as concrete as they need to be for your students to be successful.
2. Model as much language and writing as your students need.

It is now time to discuss a critically important aspect of the teaching of word writing: the area of emotional response. Many of your students will probably have experienced a great deal of failure in the past. Unless they have been in very safe and protective environments, if they have reached the fourth grade or beyond and they need instruction in word writing, they probably do not perceive themselves as successful writers.

Using *Let's Write!* offers the best antidote for past failures by providing a program where students are successful from the beginning, day after day. Feelings will come up, and sometimes students will want to talk about how much they don't like to write. One good response is to say that you are sad that they have not enjoyed writing in the past. Writing probably has been hard for them, and people usually don't like to do things that are difficult. Tell your students that you are teaching them to write in a way that will make writing easier for them.

Some students exhibit resistive behaviors about writing that make it difficult to provide instruction. They can appear passive and tired and function very slowly, or they can be outright antagonistic to writing tasks. Keep in mind that these behaviors are based on past failures. Focus on the positive in each lesson. If a student manages to write three words, praise the student for his efforts, and talk about what he has actually accomplished. For example, you could say, "I see that you've written the word 'tree' for the category 'something that grows.' I'm glad you chose that word because trees are so important to our world." You might bring in a book on rain forests the next day and do a small read-aloud on the subject.

This is not artificial teacher behavior. This interaction is based on the belief that once students feel successful and safe with writing, they will write. Especially at the word writing stage, it is critical to help students overcome their fear.

One other issue must be discussed: How do you know when your students are ready to move on from word writing to sentence writing? The basic principle is that students should be extremely comfortable with word writing before more challenge is given. When you do introduce sentence writing, your main task is to watch to see how your students respond. If they are resistive to sentence writing, return to more word writing practice.

Once students are ready, the transition to sentence writing is effortless and pleasant. Spend as much time as is needed at the word writing level to ensure that this easy transition will occur.

GRAMMAR CONCEPTS PRESENTED AT THIS LEVEL

The following two main grammar concepts should be taught at this level:

1. A **noun** is a person, place, or thing. For advanced students, the concept that a noun can be an abstract idea such as "knowledge" is also presented.
2. A **verb** is an action word. For advanced students, the concept of a verb as a passive action word such as "think" is also presented.

Refer to the "Grammar" chapter in Part Two for a more complete discussion of these concepts.

EDITING CONCEPTS PRESENTED AT THIS LEVEL

Students are asked to notice written words. Use discretion concerning how specific this should be. Some options are:

1. Notice the initial consonant sounds.
2. Notice when words have suffixes like "ed" and "ing."
3. Notice the length of words.

At this level, the noticing must be informal and relaxed. Refer to the "Editing" chapter in Part Two for a more complete discussion of this subject.

ACTIVITIES

The following activities are presented for working with writing words. Choose activities that are fun and comfortable for students. Some students like art, and this medium can be a powerful tool to help them break into writing. Others feel phobic about any writing, even when it is presented in connection with an activity they enjoy. For these students, carefully plan very short lessons where they will be asked to write no more than four or five words.

1. **Do labeling.** This can be done in many ways, for example:

   a. Students cut out pictures from old magazines that fit in a given category, for example, food. They then paste these pictures on a large piece of paper and label the category. If they wish, they can label each type of food represented.

   b. Students draw their own picture of an animal or an object. They then label the picture and its parts. An excellent series of books called *Eye-Openers* (Aladdin Books, Macmillan, New York, 1991, 1992) includes books on topics such as dinosaurs, jungle animals, and other topics. One of the books is *Cars*, written by Angela Royston, with photography by Tim Ridley, and illustrations by Jane Cradock-Watson and Dave Hopkins, car consultant and model maker—Ted Taylor, (Dorling Kindersley Limited, London, 1991). This picture book features large two-page color pictures of different types of cars. A short paragraph is written about each one, and parts of the car are labeled. For example, on the sports car pages, the headlight, seat belt, trunk, and wheel are labeled.

      Students enjoy seeing these books and then using them as a model for making their own pictures and labels. Sometimes, they like to collect their pictures in a book.

2. **Play the Category Game.** For this game, you provide categories and words that fit into them. Students have to write the words under the appropriate categories. You can start with two headings such as COLORS and THINGS YOU FIND IN A CLASSROOM. Then, list eight or ten words, all of which fit into the two groups.

   Once students are familiar with this game, they usually enjoy selecting among four categories. Sometimes, they like to make up a game for their peers. Two examples of this game are provided on pages 9 and 10. The first is appropriate for very beginning students for whom it can be helpful to present words that are easy to spell. The second focuses on content as opposed to phonetic regularity.

3. **Finish a sentence.** For this activity, you provide sentences that have one missing word. For example:

   - It had rained the night before, so there were many _____ in the streets. (puddles)

   - "I am _____ that you are feeling better," Juan said. (glad)

   - Letitia cooked the spaghetti on the _____ . (stove)

   Concerning the missing words, you can either provide a choice between two words, or you can write a series of sentences and a word list to choose from. You can also offer no words and let students think of words that fit logically in the sentence. This last option is the most challenging.

   Two examples of this activity can be found on pages 11 and 12. The first one is appropriate for very beginning students for whom it can be helpful to present words that are easy to spell. The second focuses on content as opposed to phonetic regularity.

4. **Write a word description.** Provide an interesting object and then brainstorm key words that it stimulates. Model for your students to notice not only how it looks, but also how it feels. Does it have a smell? What do you think it was used for? If you bring in food, such as a jar of cinnamon, be sure that your students are not allergic to this food if they are going to taste it. Once the brainstorming is done, ask your students to select some key words and write them down.

5. **Pantomime words.** Brainstorm with your students some words that they will like to act out. Some good possibilities are "jump," "smile," "read," "drive," and "huge." Ask your students to write each word on an index card. Once a card deck is made, one student selects a card and acts it out for the others to guess. If you are working individually with a student, you can act out words for each other.

6. **Make word collections.** Decide on a topic with your students, such as "words that relate to transportation," or "words that tell size," or "words that rhyme with 'pet.'" Provide either a basket or a box where students can place words that fit in these categories, one word per card. This can be an enjoyable group activity in which everyone cooperates to see how many words can be collected.

7. **Do interviews.** Brainstorm a series of questions with your students. Write out favorite questions for them on a sheet of paper, being careful that only one-word answers are required. Two examples are provided on pages 13 and 14.

   Students enjoy interviewing their peers and other members of the school community. They can also interview family members or other people outside of school.

8. **Make and play games.** Students who resist writing in any other form often enjoy making games. Two favorites are Concentration and Word Bingo. For the first, create a card deck by making pairs of cards. For example, write the word "music" on two separate 3″ × 5″ index cards.

    Once a deck of at least sixteen cards is ready, place the cards face down in a random order on the table. The first player selects two cards. If the words match, she keeps them and the next player has a turn. If they don't match, she replaces them face down on the table and the next player continues the game. The winner is the person with the most cards at the end.

    For Word Bingo, take a piece of 8½″ × 11″ paper and divide it into at least twelve sections. Decide on a group of game words with your students. Ask your students to select among these game words and write one per section on their game card.

    On 3″ × 5″ index cards, write the game words in a random order. Game words can be repeated on both the game boards and the index cards.

    To play the game, the caller shuffles the deck and calls the cards in order. Players cover each word called. The first player to cover all his sections wins the game.

9. **Answer riddles.** Prepare a series of "I'm thinking of" riddles. You can do these in various ways. One way is to place some objects on the table and say, "I'm thinking of something that is right before us and is red. You can drink out of it." Students write their answer, "a cup."

    The riddles can increase in complexity and abstraction. Examples of some riddles are offered on pages 15 and 16.

10. **Do fill-in-the-blanks short paragraphs and stories.** Keep these offerings simple and direct, with clear cuing as to which type of word is needed to complete a sentence. Often, students enjoy repeating a favorite selection.

    Sometimes, students like to help you make up a fill-in-the-blank paragraph or story. They dictate and you write, or you can discuss their suggestions and decide together on what the sentences will become. This can be a very rewarding activity when students are ready for it.

    Examples of fill-in-the-blank selections are offered on pages 17 and 18.

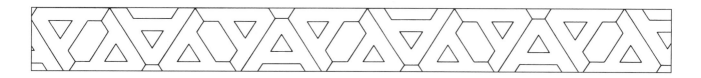

A Category Game

Choose words from your word list that belong in each category.

RELATING TO NATURE

_____

_____

_____

_____

THINGS PEOPLE DO

_____

_____

_____

_____

RHYMES WITH HAT

_____

_____

_____

PARTS OF OUR BODY

_____

_____

_____

WORD LIST

mat	pond
chin	swim
wind	at
jump	sun
rat	skin
hop	hand
hip	sit
sand	bat

Name _____   **Date** _____

A Category Game

Choose words from your word list that belong in each category.

ANIMALS

_____

_____

_____

_____

FOOD

_____

_____

_____

_____

FURNITURE

_____

_____

_____

_____

RELATING TO THE WEATHER

_____

_____

_____

_____

WORD LIST

carrot	puppy
tiger	humidity
tornado	bookcase
table	corn
bread	mouse
elephant	rain
hurricane	chair
desk	spaghetti

Name _____ **Date** _____

Find the Right Word!

Fill in the blanks with words from the word list.

1. The batter _____ the ball into left field.

2. Pedro put a _____ on the letter and mailed it.

3. A _____ of wind blew the paper away.

4. "It's so hot. Let's go for a _____ in the pool," Anna said.

5. The bird built a _____ in the tree.

6. The _____ took good care of her kittens.

7. "I'll make a big _____ of soup for supper," Tom said.

8. A _____ can live in a pond.

9. Leroy spread blueberry _____ on his toast.

10. "The festival was lots of _____," Mary said.

WORD LIST

frog	fun
pot	cat
hit	swim
nest	gust
stamp	jam

Name _____ **Date** _____

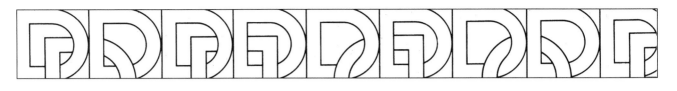

Find the Right Word!

Fill in the blanks with words from the word list.

1. _____ is the month that comes right after March.

2. "There's too much noise in here. Please be _____," Mr. Rod-riguez said.

3. The _____ is a stringed instrument.

4. Two times ten equals _____.

5. "I like to listen to _____ to relax," Beth said.

6. Le Ly took the _____ to Chicago.

7. The little girl was proud of her new front _____.

8. The _____ has very sharp quills.

9. "I will _____ a picture of that bridge," Matt said.

10. Sarah enjoys growing tomatoes in her _____.

WORD LIST

music	April
paint	garden
teeth	twenty
quiet	porcupine
train	violin

Name _____ **Date** _____

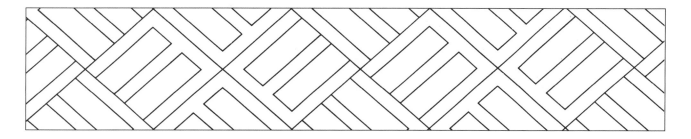

An Interview of a Fellow Student

Write the answers in the spaces provided. Remember that if the person you are interviewing does not wish to answer any question, thank the person for telling you that, and skip that question.

1. How old are you? _____

2. Where do you live? _____

3. Do you have a pet? _____ If you do, what kind of animal is he or she? _____ What is your pet's name? _____

4. What do you like best about school? _____

5. What do you like least about school? _____

6. What do you like to do during your free time? _____

7. If you could spend a week anyplace in the world, where would you go?

   _____

8. If you had plenty of money and could buy one present for yourself, what would you buy? _____

9. If you had plenty of money and could buy one present for the school, what would you buy? _____

10. Please tell me one quality that you admire in other people. _____

   _____

Name _____ **Date** _____

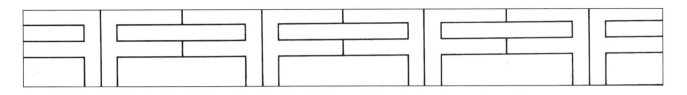

An Interview of an Adult in the School or Community

Write the answers in the spaces provided. Remember that if the person you are interviewing does not wish to answer any question, thank the person for telling you that, and skip that question.

1. Where do you live? _____

2. Where did you grow up? _____

3. What was your favorite thing to do when you were a child? _____
   _____

4. What do you like to do in your spare time right now? _____
   _____

5. What do you like to do for work? _____

6. What is your favorite kind of music? _____

7. What is your favorite food? _____

8. If you could fly, where would you fly to? _____

9. What is one thing that makes you happy in your life? _____
   _____

10. What quality do you most admire in your best friend? _____
    _____

Name _____ **Date** _____

Riddles

Answer the following riddles. There can be more than one correct answer for each riddle.

1. I'm thinking of something that is red and you can eat it.

   ANSWER: _____

2. I'm thinking of a word that rhymes with <u>and.</u>

   ANSWER: _____

3. I'm thinking of an animal that can live in a zoo and that begins with the letter <u>l.</u>   ANSWER: _____

4. I'm thinking of something that gets put in a cone and melts when it gets warm.   ANSWER: _____

5. I'm thinking of a word that has more letters than the word <u>sidewalk.</u>   ANSWER: _____

6. I'm thinking of an animal that has four paws and meows.

   ANSWER: _____

7. I'm thinking of a season of the year that usually is very hot.

   ANSWER: _____

8. I'm thinking of something that can make a mark on a piece of paper.

   ANSWER: _____

SOME POSSIBLE ANSWERS

1. apple
2. sand
3. lion
4. ice cream
5. television
6. cat
7. summer
8. pencil

Name _____   **Date** _____

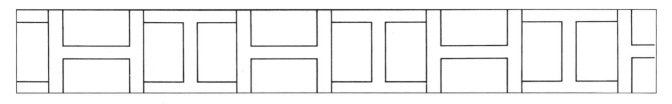

Riddles

Answer the following riddles. There can be more than one correct answer for each riddle.

1. I'm thinking of something that is green and you can sit on it.

   ANSWER: _____

2. I'm thinking of a word that has fewer letters than the word <u>ant.</u>

   ANSWER: _____

3. I'm thinking of an animal that is bigger than a tiger.

   ANSWER: _____

4. I'm thinking of something that you must have to play basketball.

   ANSWER: _____

5. I'm thinking of something that falls from the sky.

   ANSWER: _____

6. I'm thinking of an animal that is smaller than a cat.

   ANSWER: _____

7. I'm thinking of a food that you can put tomato sauce and cheese on and heat in an oven.   ANSWER: _____

8. I'm thinking of something that has two wheels and you can ride it.

   ANSWER: _____

SOME POSSIBLE ANSWERS

1. grass
2. at
3. rhinoceros
4. basketball

5. rain
6. mouse
7. pizza
8. bicycle

Name _____   **Date** _____

Fill in the Blanks

Fill in the following blanks with words that make good paragraphs.

A FASCINATING ANIMAL

A _____ is an interesting animal. He likes to sleep during

the _____. He likes to eat _____. He lives in

a _____. It's fun to know so much about _____.

A FAVORITE FOOD

One of my favorite foods is _____. I like it because it tastes

_____. It tastes _____ when it is heated up. It

tastes _____ when it is served cold. I am glad that some-

times I get to eat _____.

Name _____ **Date** _____

Fill in the Blanks

Fill in the following blanks with words that make a good story. If you want to, you can put more than one word in any blank.

John looked at the _____ on the ground. It was _____ inches long. It looked like it would feel _____ to the touch. It weighed about _____ pounds.

John felt _____. He ran to the _____. He said to his _____, "Please _____ me. There's a _____ on the ground."

John and his _____ came back and looked at the _____. Now, it was _____.

"Well, this is fascinating," John said. "I think we should _____ _____."

"I agree," his _____ said.

And they both _____.

Name _____ **Date** _____

Answer Key

A Category Game (Page 9)

RELATING TO NATURE:
    wind, sand, pond, sun

THINGS PEOPLE DO:
    jump, hop, swim, sit

RHYMES WITH <u>HAT</u>:
    mat, rat, at, bat

PARTS OF OUR BODY:
    chin, hip, skin, hand

A Category Game (Page 10)

ANIMALS:
    tiger, elephant, puppy, mouse

FOOD:
    carrot, bread, corn, spaghetti

FURNITURE:
    table, desk, bookcase, chair

RELATING TO THE WEATHER:
    tornado, hurricane, humidity, rain

Find the Right Word! (Page 11)

| 1. hit | 2. stamp | 3. gust | 4. swim | 5. nest |
| 6. cat | 7. pot | 8. frog | 9. jam | 10. fun |

Find the Right Word! (Page 12)

| 1. April | 2. quiet | 3. violin | 4. twenty | 5. music |
| 6. train | 7. teeth | 8. porcupine | 9. paint | 10. garden |

SENTENCE WRITING

Sentences are the basic building blocks of writing. Whether students are progressing up from the word writing level, or they have come to you with some good writing skills, it is important to spend time at this level. The more experience students have with sentences, the easier it will be for them to write well-organized and fluent paragraphs, reports, essays, and stories.

If you are starting with students at the sentence writing level, you must first work with them on the concepts of nouns and verbs. These were originally presented in the word writing section.

Let us first discuss how to teach sentence writing to students who have never before written a sentence. Begin with an informal assessment of these students' verbal skills. Can they verbalize sentences? Does speaking in sentences require great effort? If students are weak in this area, they first need support for the development of their verbal skills.

One good technique is to model complete sentences. Ask your students to look at you while you speak to them, and then ask them to respond in complete sentences. For example, you can say, "I like the plant on the table. Do you like the plant on the table?" (*Note:* This instruction should be done sparingly. Even with limited effort, however, it can be effective.)

A second technique is to select a good picture book for read-aloud time. After the story has been read and enjoyed, choose a few well-formed complete sentences and reread and discuss them.

A third way to help students become familiar and comfortable with verbalizing sentences is through playing the Noun Game. This game is described in the "Grammar" chapter on page 119.

One of the factors that makes writing sentences difficult is that normal conversational speech often contains incomplete sentences and improper grammar. Often, we say things like, "Want to go to the movies?" This is why, for some students, it is important to help them discover the greater formality of written English, which is required for expository writing. If a significant amount of work has been done in this area and a student is still experiencing difficulty, request that this student be given a speech and language evaluation.

HOW TO BEGIN THE ACTUAL WRITING OF SENTENCES

For students who have never written sentences or who have tried and experienced frustration, it is important to provide considerable support as they begin this work. Present this support in a three-level format:

1. For the most **basic level,** write some short sentences on the board or on large paper, such as:

- I like ice cream.
- I like the rain.
- I like cats.

Tell students that you are going to provide a model for them for part of the sentence they are going to write. Then write:

I like . . .

With a model like this, the students are, in effect, still word writing. They begin to have a sense of sentence writing, however, and gain confidence. Other possible models at this stage are phrases like:

- I don't like . . .
- My brother (sister, friend, etc.) likes to . . .
- I saw a . . .
- I have never seen a . . .
- I want to learn about . . .
- It was fun to . . .
- I am good at . . .
- It is hard to . . .
- I like to eat . . .
- Dogs are . . .
- Elephants are . . .

Notice that most of these phrases are presented in the first-person. It seems to be easiest for beginning writers to write about themselves; therefore, many of the beginning models are based on this personal approach.

2. Once your students are comfortable with the first, most basic level of support, it is time to move on to the **intermediate level** of support. Here, provide models that are less important to the content of the sentence. These models ask the students to complete the sentences with phrases as opposed to just individual words.

Some good models at this level are:

- On Saturday, I . . .
- When I'm happy, I . . .
- When I'm tired, I . . .
- My favorite kind of book is . . .
- My favorite kind of movie is . . .
- If I could talk to animals, I would . . .
- If I could fly, I would . . .
- If I were in charge of the world, I would . . .
- I like cats because . . .
- I like computers because . . .

3. The third level of support, for students who have progressed to this more **independent level,** offers models that are really sentence starters. At this level, students are not quite ready to begin writing sentences completely independently, but they are close.

Some good sentence starters are:

- I wish . . .
- If only . . .
- It's not fair that . . .
- Often, . . .
- It's good that . . .
- Yesterday, . . .
- Sometimes, . . .
- Let's . . .
- Maybe . . .
- It's funny that . . .

When students are working at this level, they often are insecure about their spelling and frequently request the proper spelling of words. The goal is for students to write freely and not stop to ask. Some students, however, are uncomfortable and feel that they really need this help. Without such assistance, they feel paralyzed. It is a judgment call concerning how much help to provide.

What often occurs is that as students become more comfortable with writing sentences, their concern over whether they have every word spelled in the standard way diminishes, and they begin to concentrate more on the content of their language. It is important for students to eventually spell correctly, but at this stage, it is better to stress content. Editing for proper spelling will begin to occur at the paragraph level.

When students are given help with spelling at the sentence level, it is most effective to provide written models, as opposed to verbally telling them the letters. This helps students gain the habit of noticing written language.

Once students don't need sentence starters to begin and are ready to write sentences totally independently, provide opportunities for them to practice their sentence writing skills. A wide variety of stimuli for practice sentences can be offered. Suggestions for these are provided in the "Activities" section of this chapter.

Some of these activities are creative, while others are not. Experiment with all types. Some students prefer the creative activities, while others feel safer with the more direct, concrete ones.

One more issue must be discussed. Some teachers feel that students who are already writing paragraphs may resist practicing their sentence writing skills. This is not often the case. If there is an individual student, however, who expresses these feelings, it can be helpful to remind the student that sentences are the basis of all written language. You can use the metaphor that professional athletes still practice sit-ups and push-ups, even though they are capable of higher athletic accomplishments.

Explain that practicing with sentence writing helps improve the fluency of their writing when they get to longer works. They will also be working on eliminating incomplete sentences from their writing.

GRAMMAR CONCEPTS PRESENTED AT THIS LEVEL

The following grammatical concepts are introduced here:

1. A sentence consists of a subject (who or what the sentence is about) and a predicate (it tells what is happening or gives information about the subject). These concepts are important because then students can understand what makes an incomplete sentence. The correct words "subject" and "predicate" are used and should not be a barrier to understanding.
2. Every sentence begins with a capital letter.
3. Every sentence ends with a punctuation mark. At this level, periods and question marks are discussed.

Refer to the "Grammar" chapter in Part Two for a more complete discussion of these concepts.

EDITING CONCEPTS PRESENTED AT THIS LEVEL

Students are held accountable for the following concepts at this level:

1. Every sentence begins with a capital letter.
2. Every sentence ends with an ending punctuation mark such as a period or a question mark.

Refer to the "Editing" chapter in Part Two for a more complete discussion of these concepts.

ACTIVITIES

The following activities provide practice for writing sentences:

1. **Write sentences using given nouns, one per sentence.** The nouns can be selected by you or student. Often, students enjoy brainstorming a list of nouns from which specific nouns can be selected.

   When students are ready, they can be given two or even three nouns to work with. Some advanced students like to challenge each other to see how many nouns they can put in one sentence.

   See "Write It With Nouns," page 28, which can be used for independent work.

2. **Write sentences using given verbs** (selected by either you or students). Start with one per sentence. Because verbs usually change form when the tenses change (as in "I kick the football" and "I kicked the football") and some verbs change in unpredictable ways (as in "I run" and "I ran"), it's important to provide support for your students with these changes. For most students who are working at this level, however, it's counterproductive to spend a great deal of time discussing these changes. It's best to help students think of the correct forms, and to treat these changes as an interesting aspect of the English language. It's not something they have to memorize.

   When students are ready, they can be given two verbs to put in a sentence. Some advanced students like to challenge each other to see how many verbs they can place in one sentence.

   See "Write It With Verbs," page 29, which can be used for independent work.

3. **Write sentences using given subjects or predicates.** This activity can be done once students are comfortable with both grammatical concepts. It is a particularly good activity to use for reinforcing students' understanding of these concepts.

   It's best to start this activity by brainstorming a list of either subjects or predicates with your students. Then, they can select ones with which to work.

   The two independent activity sheets on pages 30 and 31 offer students a chance to work with subjects and predicates.

4. **Write sentences with challenge words.** Students enjoy this activity because there is an element of friendly competition in it. You can model finding fascinating words in read-aloud selections and in other fiction or nonfiction

books. Some people have even been known to search for challenging words in the dictionary! Words can be chosen because they sound good, because they have lots of letters, because they are not well known, or simply because the person likes them.

There is a game aspect to the activity, where students like to see if they can present a word that none of their peers will know how to use. The presenting student then has to teach her friends how to use the word correctly in a sentence.

Often, it's helpful to have a special place where students can place challenge words. A shoebox or even a large piece of paper on the bulletin board where words can be collected for later use is helpful. That way, if a student finds a terrific challenge word during a time when sentences are not being written, he can record the word for future use.

See the activity sheet "Write It With Challenge Words" on page 32.

5. **Write descriptions.** For this activity, provide either an interesting object (e.g., a plastic half-lemon which is made into a button) or a picture (e.g., a huge Victorian house on the top of a deserted hill). Give students some key words for the presented stimulus. For example, for the button, the key words could be "yellow," "small," "button," "lemon," and "seeds." For the Victorian house, the words could be "huge," "deserted," "hill," "windows," and "roof."

Ask your students to write a series of descriptive sentences for each stimulus, using the key words if they wish to do so. For the button, they could write:

- It's a small button.

- The button is yellow.

- It looks like a lemon.

Once students become familiar with this activity, they enjoy repeating it with a variety of objects and pictures. They sometimes like to bring objects and pictures from home for their peers to describe.

The independent activity sheet "A Description," using a picture with key words, is provided on page 33.

6. **Write "About Me" sentences.** Beginning writers sometimes feel most comfortable writing about themselves. Provide topics and then ask your students to write sentences that describe that particular aspect of their lives. The following are some suggested queries:

- Tell me about your favorite foods.

- Tell me about an animal that you like.

- Tell me about your room at home.

- Tell me about the place you live.

- Choose a member of your family and tell me about her or him.
- Tell me about your favorite day of the week.
- Tell me about your favorite time of day.
- Tell me what you think about television.
- Tell me about a good friend.

When doing this activity, watch to see how your students react to it emotionally. If they are resistive at all or if they appear uncomfortable in any way, leave the activity and proceed to a more neutral one that does not ask them to reveal any information about their current lives. It is not always possible for us to know when students are living in difficult situations, so it is critical that we are sensitive to their reactions when such an activity is introduced. This "About Me" activity can be a powerful help to some students as they begin to learn to write, but it must be used with caution. See the two "About Me" activities on pages 34 and 35.

7. **Do interviews.** Brainstorm a series of questions with your students. Make sure that each question can be answered by a sentence, not with a word, as in the interviews in the "Word Writing" chapter.

   Ask students to select and write down their favorite questions from the brainstorm list. They then use these to interview either a peer or a member of the school or community. During the interview, they can take notes and then, later, write out the answers to the questions in complete sentences.

   Students sometimes enjoy presenting the results of their interviews to a small group. Use the "Interview" activity sheet on page 36.

8. **Write messages.** For this activity, form teams of two people each. Tell your students that no one can talk, including yourself, for a specified amount of time. Five minutes is often a good starting time.

   You can play this game in two ways:

   a. The team members have a conversation in writing. The first person asks the second a question, such as, "Do you have a pet?" or "What did you do this weekend?" The second person answers this question in a sentence. Then, he asks a question himself, and the game continues.

   b. The team members give each other directions. For example, the first person might say, "Draw a circle on this paper." The second person would do so, and then give a direction herself, for example, "Clap your hands two times."

   Any "spontaneous" conversation that arises during either of these activities must be done in writing. For example, a student might write, "I'm getting tired. I want to stop."

   You could answer, "That's fine. We'll do this again tomorrow."

9. **Write about actions.** For this activity, one person performs a specific action like opening the door. The others observe the action and then write a sentence to tell what it is. For example, they could write, "Maria opened the door."

   Students enjoy performing a large variety of actions. It can be helpful to provide such props as a baseball or a jump rope.

10. **Write questions.** These can be factual or opinion questions. The factual questions can be about all kinds of subjects, such as:

    a. facts that a student is curious about—for example, What do birds do for food when it rains?

    b. facts about a culture the student is interested in—for example, Where do the Zulu people live?

    These questions can be placed on a question board in the classroom. Ask members of your school community to participate. If anyone knows an answer or has done research to find out a fact, these can be written down for all to see.

    Students can also write opinion questions. Two examples are: What do you think about the sport of boxing? Do you think that students really learn from doing homework?

    With these questions, it's best to write one question on a sheet of paper, and then let members of the school community respond in writing. The cooperative aspect of both the factual and opinion question boards make this a powerful activity.

    One interesting variation is for students to write questions for people outside of the immediate school community. These people can be real or imaginary, such as:

    a. The President of the United States.

    b. A person who earns her living fishing.

    c. A historical figure—for example, Martin Luther King or Cleopatra.

    Possible answers to these questions can be discussed. See the independent activity sheet "Write It With Questions" on page 37.

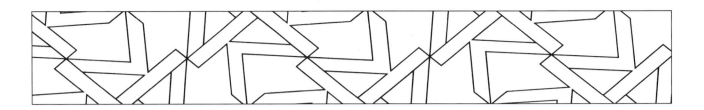

Write It With Nouns

A noun is a word that can be a person, a place, or a thing, like "student," "Australia," and "pencil." A noun can also represent an idea, like "happiness."

Write nouns on these lines:

_____   _____

_____   _____

_____   _____

_____   _____

Now, choose five nouns and use each one of them in a sentence. For example, if the noun you choose is the word "bobcat," you can write, "I saw a bobcat on TV."

1. _____

_____

2. _____

_____

3. _____

_____

4. _____

_____

5. _____

_____

Name _____   **Date** _____

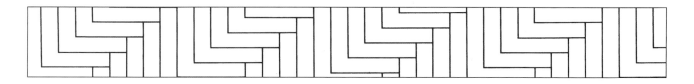

Write It With Verbs

A verb is an action word that tells what someone or something is doing. Words like "run" and "sneeze" and "think" are all verbs.

Write verbs on these lines.

_____   _____

_____   _____

_____   _____

Now choose five verbs and use each one of them in a sentence. For example, if the verb you choose is the word "chase," you can write, "The cat is chasing the dog," or "The cat chases the dog."

1. _____

_____

2. _____

_____

3. _____

_____

4. _____

_____

5. _____

_____

Name _____   **Date** _____

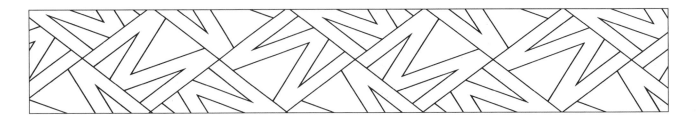

Write It With Subjects

A subject is that part of a sentence that tells who or what the sentence is about. On the lines below, you will find some subjects. Write sentences with each one.

1. After the quarterback was sacked, he _____

_____

2. The tornado _____

_____

3. The tired elephant _____

_____

4. We _____

_____

5. The swimmer _____

_____

6. His little brother _____

_____

7. The beautiful flower garden _____

_____

8. Janetta and Pam both _____

_____

9. In the spring, it _____

_____

10. The eagle _____

_____

Name _____   **Date** _____

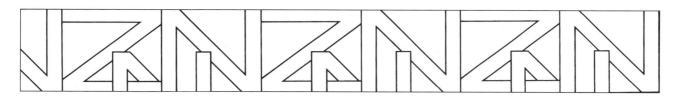

Write It With Predicates

A predicate is that part of a sentence that gives information about the subject. On the lines below, you will find some predicates. Write sentences with each one.

1. _____ walked to the beach.

2. _____ is a nice color.

3. _____ likes to play in puddles.

4. _____ jumped over the hurdles.

5. _____ ate a big pizza.

6. _____ swept the floor.

7. _____ is often late.

8. _____ had a good time at the concert.

9. _____ didn't like the cold weather.

10. _____ played chess.

11. _____ went to the movies

12. _____ was tired and sat down.

13. _____ gasped.

14. _____ flew to Arizona.

Name _____   **Date** _____

Write It With Challenge Words

Write a sentence using each of the following words. The words have been chosen because they are different or interesting or just plain silly.

1. smilet (a small smile): _____

   _____

2. palindrome (a word or group of words that is spelled the same backward

   or forward, as in the name "Hannah"): _____

   _____

3. aa (a Hawaiian word for a kind of rough lava): _____

   _____

4. hippopotomonstrosesquippedalian (a very long word that means a very

   long word): _____

   _____

5. quidnunc (someone who is very curious and is a gossip): _____

   _____

6. zloty (Polish money): _____

   _____

7. mumblecrust (someone who has no teeth): _____

   _____

8. storiology (the study of stories): _____

   _____

9. trollylolly (a kind of lace): _____

   _____

Name _____ **Date** _____

A Description

KEY WORDS

cat
sleeping
reading
book
open

Write some sentences that describe this picture. You may use the key words if you wish.

1. _____

   _____

2. _____

   _____

3. _____

   _____

4. _____

   _____

5. _____

   _____

Name _____ **Date** _____

About Me

Think about your favorite sport or hobby. Then, write some sentences about what you particularly enjoy about this activity. For instance, if your favorite sport is skateboarding, you could write:

I really like to skateboard because it's exciting to do tricks.

_____

_____

_____

_____

_____

_____

_____

_____

_____

_____

_____

_____

_____

_____

_____

_____

Name _____ **Date** _____

About Me

Write some sentences about things you would like to learn about. For example, if you would like to learn about the ocean, you could write:

I would like to learn about the fish who live in the deepest parts of the ocean.

_____

_____

_____

_____

_____

_____

_____

_____

_____

_____

_____

_____

_____

_____

_____

_____

_____

Name _____ **Date** _____

An Interview

Write the answers in the spaces provided. Remember that if the person you are interviewing does not wish to answer any question, thank the person for telling you this, and skip that question.

1. If you could plan your favorite meal, what would it be? _____
   _____

2. What is the thing that you like best about the place where you live? __
   _____

3. What do you like to do in your spare time? _____
   _____

4. Please name a hero, and then say why you admire him or her. _____
   _____

5. What would you do if you had a million dollars? _____
   _____

6. What kind of programs do you think should be on television? _____
   _____

7. If you could change one thing about all schools, what would you change?
   _____

8. If you had one wish to give the world, what would you wish for? _____
   _____

Name _____   **Date** _____

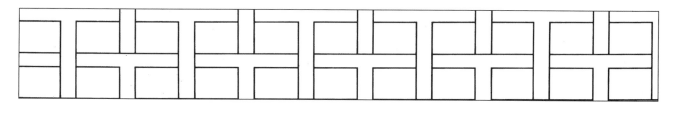

Write It With Questions

Think of a person you would like to meet. This person can be a living person or a figure from history. Then, write some questions that you would like to ask this person.

For example, here are some questions you could prepare if you wanted to meet Nelson Mandela:

How did you decide to become involved with politics?

Do you have children?

What was it like to go from prison to governing your country?

Write your questions here. Once you have finished, find some people who would like to discuss possible answers with you.

_____

_____

_____

_____

_____

_____

_____

_____

_____

_____

_____

_____

_____

Name _____   **Date** _____

PARAGRAPH WRITING

The ability to write clear, well-organized paragraphs is a huge step forward in the development of a person's writing skills. By the time the students are ready to face this new challenge in the *Let's Write!* program, they will already have written series of sentences. Writing a well-organized paragraph, however, is a unique task, and many students profit from specific instruction in this area.

Begin this instruction by teaching a specific structured paragraph consisting of a topic sentence, three supporting detail sentences, and an ending sentence. Some teachers worry that structured instruction in such a rigid form will inhibit flexibility in students' future writing, but this has not been the case with the *Let's Write!* program.

Right from the beginning, tell your students that you will be teaching them a very specific way to write paragraphs—that this is only one way to write them, and they may write paragraphs differently in the future. Tell them that this exercise will help them develop their paragraph writing skills. Once they have practiced enough and feel comfortable with this type of writing, they may write more freely. They may write more than three supporting detail sentences, for example, or they can vary the way they begin and end a paragraph.

Usually, once students have internalized the topic sentence, supporting detail sentences, and ending sentence format, they naturally move on to less guided writing. They still, however, maintain the sense of logical order that makes an easy-to-read and understandable paragraph.

Follow three specific steps in teaching paragraph writing:

1. **Discuss topics with your students.** Present some topics, such as "My Pet" or "School Worries." You can look at the ideas for lists in Appendix A and use these same categories for topics. Ask your students to give suggestions for topics, too.

Write each topic down on an index card. Once approximately five topics are given, tell your students that you are going to create sentences from these topics. For the topic, "Soccer," you could create the topic sentence, "I like to play soccer." At this stage, try to develop topic sentences that will be easy to support. Using the first person is often the most accessible for beginning paragraph writers. Write down each topic sentence on a separate index card and keep it with its topic.

38

Model the development of topic sentences as much as you need to. Continue with this activity until students are able to create their own topic sentences from a variety of topics.

More than one topic sentence can be developed for each topic. It's effective to keep these topics and their related sentences in a small box so that they can be reused in the future. They are excellent for students to look at, for example, at a future stage when they are practicing paragraph writing on their own and need some suggestions for what to write about.

2. **Tell your students that they are now going to add supporting details to their paragraphs.** Select a favorite topic sentence from your card deck of possibilities. With your students, brainstorm some sentences. For example, your topic may be "Smoking," and the topic sentence is "I think it's bad to smoke cigarettes." Some supporting detail sentences could be:

- It costs a lot of money.
- It can make you sick.
- You can get addicted to cigarettes.
- The smoke makes you smell bad.

Write all these sentences out, one to an index card. With your students, select three favorite sentences. On a piece of paper, write out the topic sentence and then the three supporting detail sentences. At this stage, label both types of sentences. Use Figure 1, "The Start of a Paragraph," or a similar format.

Have the sentences labeled and separated at this point. It helps students keep track of the purpose of each sentence in the paragraph. Using the form does not seem to inhibit students' writing paragraphs in the standard way (indent the first sentence and then have the sentences follow each other) once they are ready to do so. They seem to have more difficulty in trying to write paragraphs in the standard way when they are beginning this work.

Practice brainstorming and writing out supporting detail sentences for your students until they seem ready to do this work themselves. Then, have them practice doing the actual writing. Continue collecting new topics and topic sentences for future work.

3. **When students are secure with topic and supporting detail sentences, introduce ending sentences.** Some students have difficulty with these, because they seem too similar to the topic sentence. Model a lot of possibilities. Tell your students that this is the place where they can express their opinions, as in the following:

Topic Sentence:

Kittens are fun to have around.

Figure 1.   The Start of
a Paragraph

TOPIC SENTENCE

_____

_____

THREE SUPPORTING DETAIL SENTENCES

1. _____

   _____

2. _____

   _____

3. _____

   _____

Name _____   **Date** _____

Three Supporting Detail Sentences:

1. They pounce on anything that moves.

2. They like to be picked up and cuddled.

3. They run and jump just for the joy of it.

Ending Sentence:

I like kittens a lot.

Usually, students become more able to think up ending sentences once enough modeling and practice has been done.

Figure 2, "A Paragraph," provides a form for writing complete paragraphs. Your students should practice a great deal of paragraph writing using this form. Once they are very comfortable with it and wish to try writing in the standard way, they may do so on regular wide-lined paper. This size paper is recommended over college-ruled paper.

Some students with spatial problems have difficulty making the transition from the form to standard paragraphs. When they first try, it appears that they haven't mastered writing paragraphs at all, because they seem to have lost the five-sentence structure.

For these students, make up a form right on the wide-lined paper. Pencil in a little TS (for topic sentence), 3 DS (for three supporting detail sentences), and an ES (for ending sentence) in appropriate places. Then, work with them until they understand that they are doing the same thing they did before, just on a different kind of paper.

Once they are successful with this, begin to work with the standard paragraph structure. Show them how to indent the first sentence and then to continue, with each successive sentence following the other. It may be necessary to pencil in a little TS, and so on, on the paper. Progress from step to step slowly, only after your students are successful.

These steps are time consuming, but they help students with spatial difficulties really master writing paragraphs in any physical context. They learn that the size or shape of the paper does not affect their basic logical paragraph structure.

One other challenge that some people have must be discussed. Some students tend to free-associate when writing paragraphs. Often, these students have some type of auditory difficulty. The following technique helps students learn to stay focused in their paragraph writing.

This technique involves working with sequencing skills. To begin, you will need paragraphs that are carefully structured so that there is an obvious sequence to them. These paragraphs are written out in five strips, one sentence per strip. Use the sentence strips in Figure 3, "Paragraphs for Sequencing Skills."

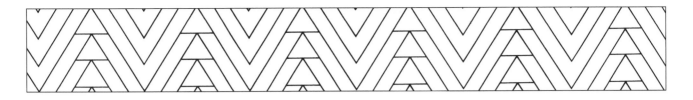

Figure 2. A Paragraph

TOPIC SENTENCE

_____

_____

THREE SUPPORTING DETAIL SENTENCES

1. _____

   _____

2. _____

   _____

3. _____

   _____

ENDING SENTENCE

_____

_____

_____

Name _____ **Date** _____

Figure 3. Paragraphs for Sequencing Skills

Follow the suggestions in the text for using the following paragraph strips.

PARAGRAPH A

— — — — — — — — — — — — — — — — — — —

Abdul cleaned the kitchen floor.

— — — — — — — — — — — — — — — — — — —

First, he swept it with a broom.

— — — — — — — — — — — — — — — — — — —

Next he washed it.

— — — — — — — — — — — — — — — — — — —

Last, he put a coat of wax on the floor.

— — — — — — — — — — — — — — — — — — —

Abdul was very proud of the job he'd done.

— — — — — — — — — — — — — — — — — — —

PARAGRAPH B

— — — — — — — — — — — — — — — — — — —

Pamela had three good meals on Monday.

— — — — — — — — — — — — — — — — — — —

For breakfast, she had pancakes.

— — — — — — — — — — — — — — — — — — —

For lunch, she had a cheeseburger and fries.

— — — — — — — — — — — — — — — — — — —

For supper, she had lasagne and salad.

— — — — — — — — — — — — — — — — — — —

Pamela did not go to bed hungry on Monday.

— — — — — — — — — — — — — — — — — — —

Figure 3.   (continued)

PARAGRAPH C

— —

This is how Celise makes a garden.

— —

She prepares the soil for the seeds.

— —

She plants the seeds in the earth.

— —

She waters the seedlings and weeds around them.

— —

By caring for her garden so well, Celise gets a terrific harvest.

— —

PARAGRAPH D

— —

This is how Joshua writes a letter.

— —

He gets some paper and a pencil.

— —

He writes his message.

— —

He puts the letter in an envelope, puts a stamp on it, and mails it.

— —

Joshua mails a lot of letters each year.

— —

Cut out the five sentence strips and place them in front of your student. Ask him to select the topic sentence out of the group. Once he has done this successfully, ask him to sequence the next four sentences in the correct order. When this is done, ask your student to tell you what purpose each sentence serves in the paragraph.

This technique is quite effective in helping students eliminate irrelevant free associations in their writing. They also enjoy the activity.

GRAMMAR CONCEPTS PRESENTED AT THIS LEVEL

The following grammatical concepts are introduced here.

1. An **adjective** is a word that describes a noun.
2. An **adverb** is a word that describes a verb.

Refer to the "Grammar" chapter in Part Two for a more complete discussion of these concepts.

EDITING CONCEPTS PRESENTED AT THIS LEVEL

Students are held accountable for the following concepts at this level:

1. Students are asked to begin to notice their spelling. Choose a spelling pattern that a student has mastered during spelling instruction. Ask this student to edit for this pattern.

   The task of selecting spelling words and patterns for which students are held accountable is very important work. Carefully choose the amount of accountability for any individual so that she is challenged but not overwhelmed. At this stage in her writing, it is better to err on the side of too little challenge than too much.
2. Most sentences, other than one-word sentences such as "Hello" or "Ouch" need a subject and predicate. Students are asked to find and correct any incomplete sentences in their writing.

   Refer to the "Editing" chapter in Part Two for a more complete discussion of these concepts.

ACTIVITIES

In the first five activities, students are asked to write paragraphs about a particular subject area. Many beginning writers feel comfortable in one or two areas, such as "Computers" or "Football." Often, however, their confidence in the scope of their knowledge is limited.

One technique that helps beginning writers greatly increase the range of what they can write about is to select good read-aloud text in interesting subject areas. Try to choose simple and clear text that gives a relatively small amount of information. One good series is the *Eyewitness Books*, (Alfred A. Knopf, 1990–1997). Each book in this series focuses on a topic such as trees, shells, music, and the ecology in ponds and rivers. Another good series, with less complex text, is the *Eyewitness Juniors* series, also published by Knopf, 1990, 1991, 1992. This series has books on such subjects as monkeys, bears, cars, and flying machines.

There are many good sources of information. Encyclopedias can be excellent. Spend some time in your local library just looking at what is available. You can develop your own list of good read-aloud text for your students. In a busy schedule with a limited book budget, your personalized list of what is locally available is invaluable. Then, for example, if there is a particularly good text on countries in Africa, you can present some excellent topics for paragraph writing in this subject area.

To use this technique most effectively, tell your students the general topic for the paragraph. Read a short selection aloud, and then discuss it. With your students, decide on a topic sentence. Then, discuss possible supporting detail sentences and ending sentences. Record these possibilities. Reread the selection if this is appropriate. Then, ask your students to write their own paragraphs.

1. **Write about people and animals.** Either present a read-aloud selection as discussed above, or write from students' experiences.

   Some good topic sentences are:

   - These are three kinds of birds that live in the rain forest.
   - Lizards are fascinating animals.
   - I admire the people of Mexico.
   - You must take good care of pets.
   - Friends are people who add a lot to your life.

   Use the independent activity sheet "Write About an Animal" on page 51.

2. **Write about things.** Either provide a good read-aloud selection as discussed above or write from students' experiences.

   Some good topic sentences are:

   - These are some trees that flower.
   - It's important to take good care of a car.
   - Computers are very useful tools.
   - This is what I have planted so far in my garden.
   - You can get a lot of information from the newspaper.

3. **Write about activities.** Either provide a good read-aloud selection as discussed above, or write from student's experiences.

    Some good topic sentences are:

- These are some team sports.

- This is what I do on Saturday.

- These are some things I like to do on a rainy day.

- It's important to observe these rules when you drive.

- Working at the post office seems to be an interesting job.

4. **Write about events or times.** Either provide a good read-aloud selection as discussed above, or write from students' experiences.

    Some good topic sentences are:

- Spring is my favorite season of the year.

- The Civil War left many scars on the people of the United States.

- Kwanzaa is an important holiday.

- I enjoy my birthday a lot.

- These important events occurred in the 1960s.

5. **Write about places.** Provide a good read-aloud selection as discussed above, or write from students' experiences.

    Some good topic sentences are:

- The Mississippi River is amazing.

- The swamp was full of many kinds of life.

- Colorado is a fascinating state.

- Here are three countries in South America.

- I have learned all these things about the desert.

6. **Write "why" paragraphs.** For this activity, propose a question that students will answer in a paragraph. You can ask, for example, "Why is it important not to eat a lot of sugar?" Students can begin their paragraphs with the topic sentence, "These are some reasons why it is important not to eat a lot of sugar."

    Some possible queries from the natural world are:

- Why are rain forests important?

- Why is exercise good for people?

- Why do some animals live in groups?

    Some possible queries that relate to individuals are:

- Why do you like to play soccer?

- Why do you want to learn to write?

- Why do you pester your little brother?

7. **Write "how-to" paragraphs.** In these paragraphs, students express how to do something, such as:

   • brush their teeth

   • change a bicycle tire

   • bounce a ball

   • plant a seed

   • wash a window

   Often, once they understand this activity, students enjoy brainstorming a list of possible topics.

   For these paragraphs, students sometimes wish to write more than three supporting detail sentences. This is acceptable, as long as they complete the paragraph with an ending sentence.

   "How-to" paragraphs can also be humorous. Students can write, for example, how to:

   • break a date

   • trip over a shoelace

   • get someone mad at you

   • be late

   • eat too much and get a stomach ache

   Use the independent activity sheet that illustrates a humorous "how-to" paragraph on page 52.

8. **Write "opinion" paragraphs.** Ask your students to write their opinions about a controversial subject. For example, you could ask, "Do you think that marijuana should be legalized?" Students begin their writing with the topic sentence, "I think that marijuana (should or should not) be legalized for the following reasons."

   Some possible queries about national and international issues are:

   • What do you think about v-chips to control what young people watch on television?

   • Is pollution a problem in the world?

   • Do you think that the United States should spend more money on public education?

   • Should motorcyclists be forced to wear helmets?

   • Should people be able to drive before the age of sixteen?

   Some possible queries at the personal and moral level are:

   • Do you think students should be expelled for cheating?

- What do you think about homework? Is it usually a valuable learning tool or a waste of time?

- Do you think people should ever lie to each other?

- What do you think about bullies?

- What do you think is the best way to help a friend who is unhappy?

As with all activities with emotional content, it is important to be sensitive to your students' reactions. If they appear uncomfortable, quickly introduce a new, less threatening activity.

Use the independent activity sheet "An Opinion Paragraph" on page 53.

9. **Write "what if" paragraphs.** For this activity, present a "what if" possibility, and ask students to write a paragraph about it. For example, you could ask, "What if you could fly? What would you do?" Students begin their work with, "This is what I would do if I could fly."

Some possible "what ifs" are:

- What if you could play basketball as well as Michael Jordan?

- What if you could turn copper into gold?

- What if you were Superwoman?

- What if you were a polar bear?

- What if you were a detective?

- What if you won the lottery?

- What if you were in charge of the world?

- What if you traveled back in time to the dinosaur age by accident?

- What if you met Bigfoot?

The independent activity sheet "A What If Paragraph" is provided on page 54.

10. **Write a "Can You Beat This?" paragraph.** This is an enjoyable activity in which writers get to exaggerate excessively. Provide a topic such as "My cat is the smartest cat in the world." Then, challenge your students to write the most outrageous paragraph they can to show everyone how their cat really is the smartest.

Other topics are:

- My computer is the fastest computer.

- My dog is the largest dog in this town.

- I ate more than anyone else for dinner.

- I can jump the highest of anyone.

- My friend Tanya has the strangest looking car in the world.

Use the independent activity sheet "A Can You Beat This? Paragraph" on page 55. Even if you are going to do this activity in class and will use a different topic from the one shown, it's helpful to read aloud the sample paragraph as a model.

11. **Write a "Find the Lies" paragraph.** Writers begin this paragraph with the topic sentence, "Here are some interesting facts about me." They then write some supporting detail sentences, one or more of which may be a lie. When the paragraphs are written, they challenge other people to find any lies that may be present.

This activity may be varied to "Find the Lies" in a subject area—for example, airplanes. Students can include one or more lies and then challenge others to find the lies. Use the independent activity sheet "A Find the Lies Paragraph" in a subject area, found on page 56.

12. **Play a description game.** For this activity, you need several of a similar object—for example, some sea shells, pebbles, books, or marbles. Place the objects on the table in front of your students.

Each student mentally selects one of the objects. He then writes a paragraph to describe his object, including its unique aspects.

When all the paragraphs are written, every student reads aloud her own. If the others are able to identify the particular object chosen, the student gets a point.

This activity can be repeated. Often, students like to contribute groups of items for this game. An ongoing score sheet can be kept that will, in time, establish a champion description writer.

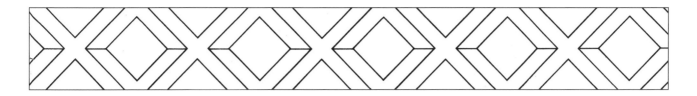

Write About an Animal

Here is a paragraph about a tarantula.

   Tarantulas are very interesting spiders. There are about thirty different kinds of tarantulas in the United States. Tarantulas have eight legs. Their bite is about as poisonous as that of a bee. Some people think that tarantulas are so interesting that they keep them as pets.

   Choose an animal that is as interesting as the tarantula, and write a paragraph about that animal here.

_____

_____

_____

_____

_____

_____

_____

_____

_____

_____

_____

_____

_____

_____

_____

Name _____   **Date** _____

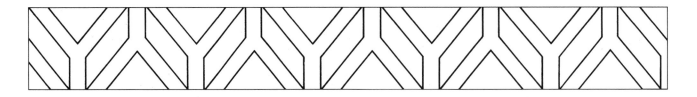

A "How-To" Paragraph

Think for a minute about how you would feel if, one day, you forgot to do your homework (even though this never actually happens). Write a paragraph explaining how you didn't get into trouble for this mistake.

Here is one example of a paragraph:

This is how I didn't get into trouble when I forgot to do my homework. First, I went up to my teacher, looking very apologetic and upset. Next, I told her how I'd been captured by aliens and had just been returned to school. Last, I promised to do my homework right away, without delay. I didn't get into trouble this time, but I don't think I'll try it again.

_____

_____

_____

_____

_____

_____

_____

_____

_____

_____

_____

_____

_____

_____

Name _____   **Date** _____

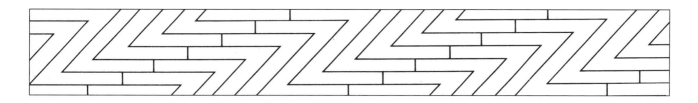

An Opinion Paragraph

Write a paragraph about what you think about television. Here is one example:

    I think that watching television can be good. You can learn a lot from science and nature programs. You can see great old movies. Sometimes, you can just watch something silly and relax. I think it's okay to watch TV, as long as you don't watch it too much.

_____

_____

_____

_____

_____

_____

_____

_____

_____

_____

_____

_____

_____

_____

_____

Name _____ **Date** _____

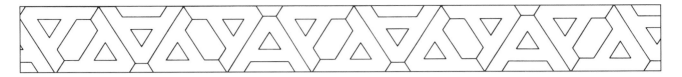

A "What If" Paragraph

What would you do if you woke up one morning to find an elephant sitting next to you on your bed? Write a paragraph like the one below to say what you would do.

    This is what I would do if I woke up one morning to find an elephant sitting on my bed. First, I would ask him very politely to get up. Then, I'd try to give him a little shove. If he still didn't move, I'd run for help. I don't know if any of these would work, but that's what I'd do.

Name _____   **Date** _____

A "Can You Beat This?" Paragraph

Write a paragraph that begins with the topic sentence, "Saturday was the most boring day of my life." Try to exaggerate even more than in the following paragraph.

Saturday was the most boring day of my life. I was so bored, I counted the hairs on my head. Then, I copied the dictionary for excitement. By Saturday evening, I was so bored that I went outside and played a game of baseball all by myself. Saturday was a gold-medal boring day.

_____

_____

_____

_____

_____

_____

_____

_____

_____

_____

_____

_____

_____

_____

_____

_____

_____

Name _____   **Date** _____

A "Find the Lies" Paragraph

The following paragraph may not contain "all and nothing but the truth."
See if you can find any lies.

Massachusetts is an interesting state. It is in the northeast part of the
United States. Its capital is Springfield. It was one of the original thirteen
colonies. These are just a few facts about Massachusetts.

Now choose a state and write a paragraph about it that may contain one
or more lies. When you're finished, see if your friends can find any lies.

Name _____   **Date** _____

WRITING RESEARCH REPORTS

Research reports are a valuable learning tool because, when they are approached well, students enjoy writing them. In this section, the traditional research report will be discussed. For these reports, students seek information from outside sources such as books, magazines, and people. They then select the data they wish to include and present this information using their own organization and words.

There are many excellent variations and alternatives to traditional reports. *Let's Write!* provides specific instruction on the traditional report form for two reasons, however.

1. The form provides a good structure that helps students organize data.
2. In their school careers, most students are asked at some point to write a traditional report. It helps them to have some background for this work.

When students are beginning to write reports, allow them to select topics that interest them. At times, availability of good books is a problem, especially if a student is interested only in an obscure topic. This problem is intensified if the student's reading and writing skills are limited, and the only books available are complex, sophisticated texts.

Prior to the beginning of report writing, discuss with your students some topics that interest them. Then, go to your library and select appropriate books. Bring these books back and allow your students to select their topics from the presented books.

If students are very motivated to write on a topic for which information is not easily available, tell them that you will keep searching for data. Ask them and their peers to keep looking, also. They can ask other teachers or friends, or people in their families. This search can be a valuable and satisfying part of their work. Until the new data sources are available, however, ask students to select other topics for practice reports.

Students can write reports at any level of their writing development, and it's important to have them do it because it is such a motivating activity. For many students, report writing feels like "real-life" work, and when they have completed a project, they feel that they have accomplished something important.

THE FOUR LEVELS OF REPORT WRITING

1. Students should write reports at the level at which they are comfortable. The **first, most basic level** is for students who are working on **word writing skills.** These students can provide two types of information in their reports:

- lists
- artwork with labeling

If, for example, a student is doing a report on European settlers in New England in the 1700s, this student could write lists of "things the people wore," or "food the people ate." They could draw a picture of a dwelling and label the parts. They could cut out pictures that deal with the time from magazines, and label what the pictures represent. Two independent "Report on a Place" activity sheets that illustrate the use of lists and artwork with report writing are provided on pages 64 and 65.

For reports at this beginning level, it's best to include a combination of these techniques. Students enjoy having several pages of information they can share with their peers.

Sometimes, a beginning student seems to stay at this early report writing stage for longer than is comfortable for the teacher. Even if the student is doing some sentence writing at other times, he or she still wants to stay at the word writing stage for report writing. Teachers sometimes worry that we are not challenging this student enough.

Students will usually progress to the next level once they feel comfortable with challenge. If you suspect that a student needs encouragement to go on, you can show him or her the next level and offer your assistance. Unless the student responds with enthusiasm, however, it is usually most productive to allow her or him to continue working at the stage that feels safe.

2. The **second level** is for students who are working on **sentence writing skills.** At this level, you will provide one main topic sentence, which gives a general direction. For example, if your student is writing about helicopters, give him a topic sentence like, "Here are some interesting facts about helicopters." He then writes a series of statements about helicopters. Four independent activity sheets—"Write About Animals," "Write About Places," "Write About People," "Write About Amazing Facts"—illustrate the second level of report writing. They are found on pages 66–69.

As with all levels of reports, artwork can be added as well as appropriate lists. For the helicopter report, for example, the student could draw and label the parts of a helicopter, and list the special uses for this type of airplane.

3. The **third level** is for students who are working on **paragraph writing skills.** Here, you help students establish three or more good topic sentences for their reports. To do this, first discuss what type of information students want to cover in their reports. If, for example, a student is writing a report on the continent of Africa, she may say that she wants to talk about three things: the different countries, some of the languages, and the many types of climates in the continent. Give this student three pieces of paper. Encourage her to write a topic sentence for each area on the top of each page. For example, she could write:

- The following are some different countries in Africa.
- Here are some of the languages people speak in Africa.
- There are many different climates in Africa.

Help your student begin to write paragraphs that follow the lead of the topic sentence. (Often, these paragraphs contain more than three supporting detail sentences.) Then, give your student time to work independently. Three activity sheets are provided on pages 70–72 for students working at this level: "Write About an Object of the Future," "Write About an Imaginary Place," and "Write an Autobiography."

4. The **fourth level** is for students who are **able to write paragraphs independently,** and who are ready to practice these skills. For these students, you will present the following report structure:

- An opening paragraph tells what the report will be about.
- Several paragraphs then present information.
- A finishing paragraph draws conclusions and makes comments about the topic being studied.

This format will be familiar to students, because it follows the same structure as the basic paragraph.

Three techniques can be used to help students understand this structure:

- the outline.
- pieces of lined paper labeled with the kind of text to be placed on each sheet. For example, one sheet will be for the introduction, several others will be for the information of the report (each one of these will have a main topic sentence), and one sheet will be for the conclusion.

- colored-coded index cards. For example, the introductory statements can have red dots, the information-giving statements can have green dots, and the concluding statements can have yellow dots. For this system, students write one sentence per card and then gather cards together into appropriate piles.

These three techniques are presented here because students differ in their abilities to relate to them. For some students, the outline works just fine. Others understand either the sheet system or the card system best. Experiment to find which one works best for each student.

TWO ISSUES

With all levels of report writing, students sometimes have difficulty gleaning information from books. They may be overwhelmed and have trouble choosing what they want to include, or they may have difficulty stating the information in their own words.

Once you have determined that the source material is at an appropriate level, provide as much support as is needed. You can show your students how you would begin. You can do a little cooperative writing if that seems necessary. Students need a great deal of emotional support with all types of writing, but they especially need this help when they are beginning report writing.

Have students share their reports if they wish to do so. This can be done by binding the reports and putting them on the school bulletin board or in the library. Students can also either read or talk about their reports at class meetings.

POSSIBLE WRITING TOPICS

Spend some time in your local library looking at the nonfiction books. You can also ask other teachers, friends, students, parents, and anyone who is interested if they have good nonfiction books to lend to your classroom. Tag sales and used book stores also, at times, offer some good, inexpensive books.

The possible topics for report writing are unlimited. The following general areas have been effective with students. They are offered as suggestions.

1. **Write about animals.** Most students are interested in some kind of animal, whether cats, spiders, snakes, or tigers. This area, therefore, makes an excellent first choice for beginning report writers. Also, facts about animals

tend to be clearly stated, and many books present animals in a noncomplex way. Use independent activity sheet "Write About an Animal" for writers working at the sentence level (page 64).

2. **Write about places.** This subject area is a second excellent choice for beginning report writers. Places are by nature concrete. Whether they are planets or countries or states, there are many books containing clearly delineated facts about them. Often, these books have excellent pictures students can study. Three independent activity sheets are provided on pages 65, 66, and 67. The first two, "Report on a Place," are for writers working on word writing skills, and the third, "Write About Places," is for writers working on sentence writing skills.

3. **Write about things.** Some students are fascinated by computers, while others love cars or clothing. Many books at beginning reading levels present information about things, like "trucks." At more advanced levels, students can check encyclopedias and other books for good information.

   In this subject area, there are special interest books that students can really enjoy. For example, *Extraordinary Origins of Everyday Things* by Charles Panati (Harper and Row, 1987) tells about the beginnings of such objects as the brown paper bag and sneakers, as well as selected sayings and customs. Advanced students might want to study this book and use the information in it to write a report.

4. **Write about a person.** If the person is famous, encyclopedias and other books can provide valuable information. If he or she is not famous, interviews can be conducted to learn about the person. Suggested formats for interviews are on pages 13, 14, and 36 in the "Word Writing" and "Sentence Writing" chapters. These or others created especially for the occasion can be used.

   The independent activity sheet "Write About a Person," page 68, can be used for a report on a famous person. This activity is for students working on sentence writing skills.

5. **Write about cultures.** In this area, a group of people is studied. Books can be referred to, as well as individuals who may have direct experience of the culture. Various aspects of the life of the group are researched.

   Another way to do reports in this area is to take a general subject like "food" or "houses." Here, one or more cultures are studied to compare and contrast how the people live.

   When students are doing reports on cultures, it's rewarding to host an "event." Two ideas for this are an art show of drawings of different types of homes from diverse cultures, and a food fair.

6. **Write about events.** Reports in this area tend to be somewhat challenging. When students are ready, however, they enjoy them greatly. A few key words

help. Tell students to include "what" happened, "where" it happened, "when" it happened, and "why" it happened. They can also include information, and their own good opinions, of what were some of the "effects" of the event.

7. **Write about amazing things.** Subjects such as the Loch Ness monster, UFOs, and ghosts, as well as little known facts about ordinary things, always fascinate.

    Select a number of good books on the subject from your library and place them on the table in front of your students. Sometimes, it's enjoyable to do a group report on interesting phenomena, with each person contributing information on a particular subject. If you like, once the group report is done, you can invite another group of students to come to a "Weird Reading," where all your amazing facts are shared. Students like making interesting invitations for these events.

    The independent activity sheet "Write About Amazing Facts," on page 69, is for students working at the sentence writing level.

8. **Write a report on an object of the future.** For this report, a great deal of imagination is involved. Have your students imagine an object they would like to design. For example, they can invent something new, such as a machine that will clean the air of pollution—or they can improve on an existing object, such as making an automobile of the future.

    For their reports, students must refer to books and people to help them learn what is necessary for the development of their object. They then, with artwork and writing, tell what the object does, what special features it possesses, who will use it, and so on. Students enjoy sharing their objects of the future. The independent activity sheet on page 70 illustrates a report on an object of the future. This is for students who are working on paragraph writing skills.

9. **Write about an imaginary place.** For this report, students invent a place. This can be a "new" continent, a cave community in a hidden desert, or a city populated by intelligent fish in the deepest part of the ocean.

    Students first check books and other resources to see what defines a place. They then do such artwork as maps and dioramas. For their narrative, they can include information on the climate, the terrain, any architectural structures, any resident population, and so on. The opportunities for imaginative reports in this area are unlimited. The independent activity sheet, "Write About an Imaginary Place," page 71, is for students working at the paragraph writing level.

10. **Write an autobiography.** What subject do you know more about than yourself? If students wish to do this kind of report, they often profit from some help with structuring it. You can refer them to the suggested interview ques-

tions on pages 13, 14, and 36 in the "Word Writing" and "Sentence Writing" sections for guidance. You can also ask them questions about areas of their lives that they wish to include.

As with all writing that asks students to divulge personal information, you must be very careful that students are comfortable with this. This kind of report should not be made a class assignment. It's important not to put pressure of any kind on students to "try" to write an autobiography. The students who are comfortable with this report will be enthusiastic. Others should be encouraged to choose among the many other topics available to them.

The independent activity sheet "Write an Autobiography," on page 72, is for students working on paragraph writing skills.

Write About an Animal

Choose an animal you want to study. Look at books or magazines and collect some interesting facts.

For example, if you want to study elephants, you can get a book like *Elephants* by N. S. Barrett (*Picture Library* series, Franklin Watts, 1988). Look at the pictures and read this book. Then, write some interesting facts like the following:

- There are African elephants and Indian elephants.
- A big African elephant can eat over 400 pounds of food a day.
- Elephants are good swimmers.

Write facts about your animal here.

_____

_____

_____

_____

_____

_____

_____

_____

_____

_____

_____

_____

Name _____ **Date** _____

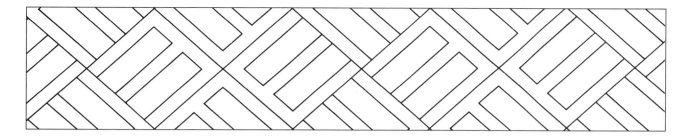

Report on a Place

Think about the place you are studying. Then pretend that you are a mouse looking at a small part of it. Draw a picture of what you (as a mouse) see. Draw your picture here.

Name _____   **Date** _____

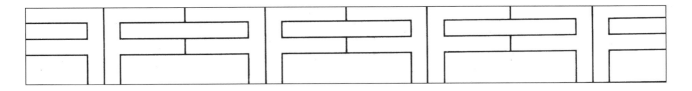

Report on a Place

Make a list of things that grow in the place you are studying. These can be types of vegetation; don't forget that people and animals are also known to grow.

_____

_____

_____

_____

_____

_____

_____

_____

_____

_____

_____

_____

_____

_____

_____

_____

_____

Name _____ **Date** _____

Write About Places

Choose a place that you would like to study. Look at books or talk to people to gain information about your place.

For example, if you want to study Puerto Rico, you could read a book like *Puerto Rico* (from the series *Cultures of the World*), by Patrica Levy (Marshall Cavendish, 1994). Look at the pictures and read this book. Talk to people who may know something about Puerto Rico. Then, write interesting facts like the following:

- Puerto Rico is over 100 miles long.
- The Taino people lived in Puerto Rico before the Spanish came.
- Two common foods are rice and beans.

Write facts about your place here.

_____

_____

_____

_____

_____

_____

_____

_____

_____

_____

_____

_____

Name _____   **Date** _____

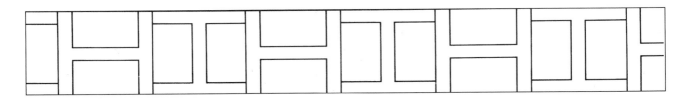

Write About a Person

Choose a person you want to study. Look at books or magazines, or talk to people to gain information about your person.

For example, if you wish to study Kareem Abdul-Jabbar, you can get a book like *Kareem Abdul-Jabbar* by Helen Borrello, introduction by Chuck Daly (Chelsea House, 1994). Look at the pictures and read this book. Then, write interesting facts like the following:

- Kareem liked music and baseball when he was a boy.
- Kareem is 7 feet and 2 inches tall.
- Kareem was an excellent student in high school.

Write facts about your person here.

_____

_____

_____

_____

_____

_____

_____

_____

_____

_____

_____

_____

Name _____ **Date** _____

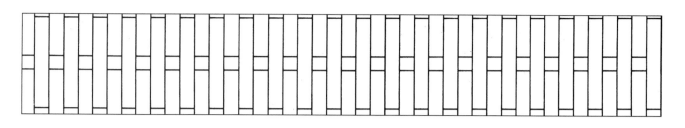

Write About Amazing Facts

Our world is filled with curious things. Talk to people and look at books and magazines to discover some amazing facts.

One good book to read is *Animalamazing* by Judith Herbst (Atheneum, 1991). In this book, you will discover the following facts:

- Animals sometimes act strangely before earthquakes.
- Salamanders can grow back their tails.
- The arctic tern migrates 20,000 miles a year.

Write some of your amazing facts here.

_____

_____

_____

_____

_____

_____

_____

_____

_____

_____

_____

_____

_____

Name _____   **Date** _____

Write About an Object of the Future

Imagine that you are designing something fabulous for the future, such as a pair of ice skates that never let you fall. As you begin your report about this special thing, you will need some good topic sentences. If you were writing about the ice skates, for example, two topic sentences could be:

- This is what the ice skates look like.
- This is how the ice skates work.

Once you have decided what object you will invent, think of some good topic sentences for your report. Write your topic sentences here.

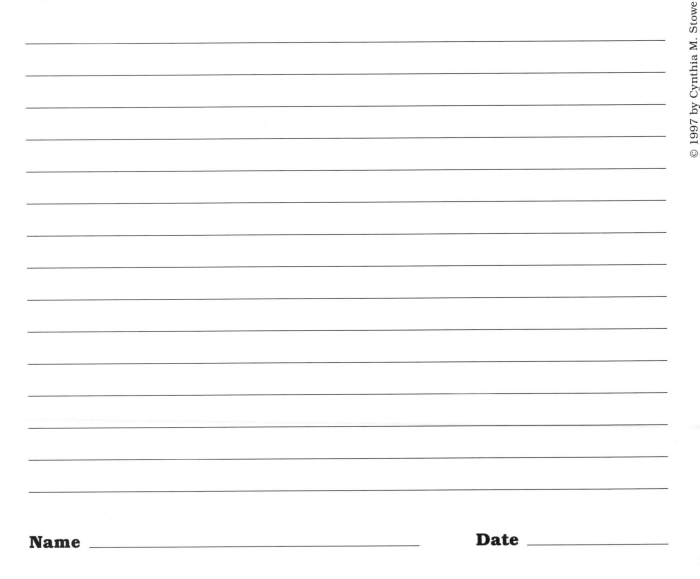

Name _____   **Date** _____

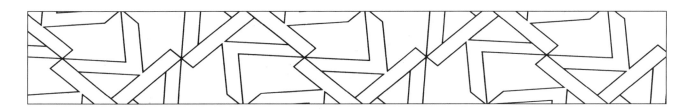

Write About an Imaginary Place

Make up an imaginary place, such as a hidden castle that exists in the center of an unknown forest. When you begin writing about your place, you will need some good topic sentences. If you were writing about the castle, for example, two good topic sentences would be:

- This is how large the castle is.
- This is who lives in the castle.

Write some good topic sentences for your imaginary place here.

_____

_____

_____

_____

_____

_____

_____

_____

_____

_____

_____

_____

_____

_____

Name _____   **Date** _____

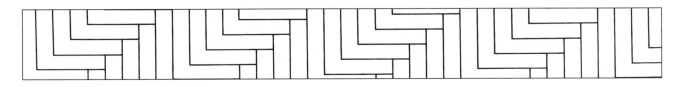

Write an Autobiography

If you want to write a report about yourself, you must figure out the kind of information you want to include. Two good topic sentences would be:

- The following people are members of my family.
- I enjoy doing many things.

Write some good topic sentences for your autobiography here.

_____

_____

_____

_____

_____

_____

_____

_____

_____

_____

_____

_____

_____

Name _____ **Date** _____

WRITING BOOK REPORTS

Working on book reports can be a profitable learning experience for students. If students have read a good book, they often enjoy sharing it. They can also profit from the writing experience that book reports provide.

Let's Write! focuses on fiction rather than nonfiction books. There is no reason, however, for students not to write reports on the latter if this genre interests them and helps them academically.

There are two ways to approach this genre of writing:

1. **Traditional book reports** in which students relate information such as the setting, plot, and characters of a story. Students' opinions about the book are often asked in these reports, but the focus is on factual accounting.
2. **Alternatives to the traditional form** which focus less on the facts and more on the interpretation of the story. Often, many different modalities, such as art and drama, are used in these alternatives.

Use discretion in deciding which type of book report is best for individual students. Some students feel comfortable with the structure of the traditional form. These students often need practice in literal fact reporting, and they feel great satisfaction when they are able to relate this information successfully.

Other students, however, find the traditional report too structured. They don't enjoy repeating facts they already know, and the traditional form spoils their enjoyment of the book.

Take your students' feelings, as well as their academic needs, into account as you make your decision about which type of book report to use. Both provide good writing experience.

TRADITIONAL BOOK REPORTS

As with research reports, students can work at four levels.

The **first level** is for students working on word writing skills. For these students, provide a series of questions that can be answered in a word or two. Use the first "Book Report" activity sheet on pages 77–78.

The **second level** is for students working on sentence writing skills. Here, provide questions that stimulate sentence writing. Use the second "Book Report" activity sheet on pages 79–80.

The **third level** is for students working at the paragraph writing stage. Provide questions which require students to write paragraphs. Use the third "Book Report" activity sheet on pages 81–82.

The **fourth level** is for students who can write paragraphs independently, and who are practicing with these skills. For these students, provide some guidance as to what type of information should be included in a good book report. Talk with your students and brainstorm a list of possible areas to cover. Help them develop some good topic sentences. Then, allow your students to choose what they feel is important to address and give them time to work independently.

10 BOOK REPORT ACTIVITIES

An unlimited number of alternatives to traditional reports is available. One excellent list of fifty of them can be found in *The Reading Teacher's Book of Lists*, 3rd ed. by Edward Bernard Fry, Jacqueline E. Kress, and Dona Lee Fountoukidis (Prentice Hall, 1993). The alternatives listed here are particularly recommended for students with special needs.

1. **Write lists.** These lists can be of general topics, such as people, animals, or places mentioned in the book. They can also be more specific to a particular story. For example, students could write a list of the Spanish words present in *The Red Comb* by Fernando Picó, the story of a runaway slave in Puerto Rico. As a second possibility, students could make a list of the things that make them laugh in *Bunnicula: A Rabbit Tale of Mystery* by Deborah and James Howe, the story of a (possibly) vampire bunny. They could also write a list of the other things Charlotte could have written in her web in *Charlotte's Web* by E. B. White, the story of the pig who was saved by a spider.

   As you can see, these lists can range from literal to highly imaginative. They can also be lists of words, phrases, or whole sentences. See the activity sheet "A List" on page 83.

2. **Make a poster for the book.** These can be displayed in the classroom with great pride.

   If students are writing a report on a picture book (and this is an interesting option as there are many sophisticated picture books that are appropriate for all levels) they can try to duplicate the style of the illustrator for their posters. One fascinating book to do this with is *The Stonecutter: A Japanese Folktale,* written and illustrated by Gerald McDermott.

3. **Make a book jacket for a paperback book.** Show students several paperback book jackets. Discuss the art on the front cover and the writing on the back that tells about the story. Then talk about the excerpts from reviews that sometimes are written on the back.

   Students can include some or all of these features, depending on their writing levels.

4. **Make games.** This is a particularly enjoyable "book report" for students. The games can be simple, like Bingo, where students place important words or characters from the book as the words to be called and covered. A second simple possibility is Concentration, where important words or characters from the book are matched.

   A favorite game, however, is the Time Line game. Here, students make a game board by drawing a large meandering line on a piece of paper. Two circles indicate START and STOP, and then students create a series of spaces from their original line. The game board will look something like this:

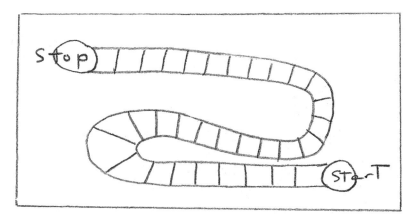

Students select a certain number of spaces (ten to fifteen is good) and write out incidents from the book, one event per space. Each event has a consequence. For example, for a game board for *Ben and Me,* the following could be written:

• Amos gets shocked. Go back five places.

• Ben goes to France. Go ahead seven places.

All incidents are written in the sequence in which they occur in the book.

Once the game board is completed, players roll the dice to see how far they will advance on each turn. It's a matter of luck as to who gets to the end first and wins the game.

5. **Write a menu for a meal one of the characters would eat.** This activity is particularly appropriate for books set in other cultures, and for historical fiction. Students may be able to find enough information about meals in their books, or they may need to do further research. This activity is potent, because thinking about what characters would eat helps them come alive in a very real way for students.

6. **Write a testimonial.** This is a good activity for books that your students have really enjoyed. Ask them to pretend that they are trying to sell the book to a person who lives far away. They must write something that will make the person run right out and buy it. The independent activity sheet "Write a Testimonial" can be found on page 84.

7. **Do a TV news interview.** This activity is particularly good for adventure stories.

   The basic format is that an interviewer asks a main character a series of questions about what has happened in the story. This is done as a class presentation.

   The student doing the book report prepares a series of questions and answers. The former are written and the latter are usually prepared to be given orally. The student then finds a friend who is willing to act as interviewer and, together, they present the interview, with the friend reading the questions. If possible, it's a lot of fun to use whatever props or costumes can be created.

   Have students use the independent activity sheet "Questions for a TV News Interview" on page 85.

8. **Write a letter to the author of the book.** This can be sent to the author at the publisher's address. Many authors will respond to letters they receive—an added bonus to this activity.

9. **Write a letter to the editor.** This letter will express a student's opinion either about what happened in the book or about a situation that is portrayed. As an example of the latter, a student could write a letter about the institution of slavery after reading *The Slave Dancer* by Paula Fox (Bradbury, 1973).

   Prepare your students by showing them two or three letters to the editor from a local newspaper. Then, let them express their opinions.

10. **Write a diary of a character, beginning after the story has ended.** Help students to brainstorm about what might happen immediately, as well as to think about how the character might feel about the ensuing events. As with real diaries, people talk about what happened in the past, so the character might divulge some fascinating insights into how he or she felt about the occurrences in the book. Use the "Write a Diary" independent activity sheet on page 86.

A Book Report

What is the title of the book? _____

_____

Who is the author? _____

_____

List some important characters. _____

_____

_____

_____

_____

_____

_____

Where does the story take place? _____

_____

When does the story take place? _____

_____

Is the story realistic, or is it a fantasy? _____

_____

Is the story serious, or is it a comedy? _____

_____

Is there a lot of action in the story? _____

_____

A Book Report (continued)

List some words that come to mind when you think of this story. _____

_____

_____

_____

_____

_____

_____

_____

_____

_____

_____

_____

_____

_____

_____

Is there anything you would like to change about this story? If so, what is it?

_____

_____

Would you recommend this story to your friends? _____

On a scale of one to ten, how would you rate this book? _____

Name _____   **Date** _____

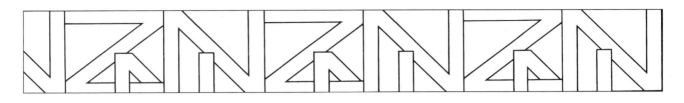

A Book Report

Answer all the questions below. When you can, please use complete sentences.

What is the title of the book? _____

_____

Who is the author? _____

_____

List some important characters. _____

_____

_____

_____

_____

Where does the story take place? _____

_____

When does the story take place? _____

_____

What is the story about? Write at least three sentences. _____

_____

_____

_____

_____

A Book Report (continued)

How did reading this book make you feel? _____

_____

_____

_____

If you could, would you change anything about this story? What would you

change, and why? _____

_____

_____

_____

What did you think about the ending of this book? _____

_____

_____

_____

What is the thing you'll remember most about this book? _____

_____

_____

_____

Write about your favorite part of the book. _____

_____

_____

_____

_____

Would you recommend this book to your friends? Why or why not? ____

_____

_____

_____

Name _____ **Date** _____

A Book Report

Answer the following questions. When you can, please use complete sentences.

What is the title of the book? _____

_____

Who is the author? _____

List some important characters._____

_____

_____

_____

_____

_____

Where does the story take place? _____

_____

When does the story take place? _____

_____

Write a paragraph that tells what the story is about. _____

_____

_____

_____

_____

_____

A Book Report (continued)

Write a paragraph that tells what you will remember most about this book.

_____

_____

_____

_____

_____

_____

_____

_____

If you could change anything about this story, what would you change?

_____

_____

Write a paragraph that tells why you would or would not recommend this

book to your friends. _____

_____

_____

_____

_____

_____

_____

_____

Name _____ **Date** _____

A List

Make a list of the different ways people and animals get from one place to another in the book you have just read. First, write down all the ways you remember, such as walking and taking a bus. Then go back to the book and see if you can find other ways of moving.

_____

_____

_____

_____

_____

_____

_____

_____

_____

_____

_____

_____

_____

_____

_____

_____

_____

_____

_____

Name _____ **Date** _____

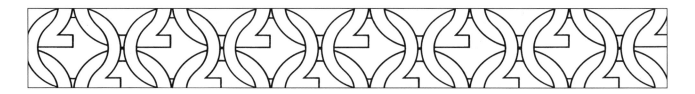

Write a Testimonial

Write a rave review of a book you have really enjoyed. Remember, you want to be so enthusiastic that people will run right out and get the book.
   You could start this way:

   This is the most fabulous, terrific book I've ever read. I laughed. I cried. I was at the edge of my seat the whole time I was reading.

   Write your review here:

_____

_____

_____

_____

_____

_____

_____

_____

_____

_____

_____

_____

_____

_____

_____

Name _____ **Date** _____

Questions for a TV News Interview

You and a friend are going to present a TV news interview. You will pretend to be a main character in a book you've just read, and you will find a friend to be the interviewer.

Prepare some questions for your friend to ask "you." For example, if you were pretending to be Julie of *Julie of the Wolves* by Jean Craighead George (illustrated by John Schoenherr, Harper and Row, 1972), the story of the Eskimo girl Miyax (Julie) who gets lost in the Arctic, your interviewer might ask:

How did you feel when you first saw the pack of wolves?

Write your questions here.

_____

_____

_____

_____

_____

_____

_____

_____

_____

_____

_____

_____

_____

Name _____ **Date** _____

Write a Diary

Write a diary for a character. "Your" diary will begin at the end of the story you have just read. For example, if you were writing a diary for Artemis Slake, the hero of *Slake's Limbo* by Felice Holman (Scribner, 1974), the story of the thirteen-year-old boy who lives alone in the city, your diary might begin:

I left that hospital because I wanted to be free. I was too afraid to go to a foster home.

Start "your" diary here.

_____

_____

_____

_____

_____

_____

_____

_____

_____

_____

_____

_____

_____

_____

Name _____ **Date** _____

WRITING STORIES

The writing of stories must be a joyful experience if students are going to profit from it. Students vary greatly in their abilities and interests in this area. Just as some people enjoy reading fiction while others prefer nonfiction, some people like to write fiction and others do not. Three different groups will be discussed in this chapter:

1. Students who dislike story writing.
2. Students who want to write stories, but who have a lot of trouble getting started and continuing to work.
3. Students who love writing stories and who can work independently once they have started.

Some students really don't like to write fiction. These students can be bright and capable in many academic areas, but using their imaginations to create worlds from words just does not appeal to them. These same people can be very creative in art, music, or other media.

Make sure that a student has a true preference for nonfiction writing, and that her resistance is not based on fear of fiction writing or unhappy experiences from the past. Offer some activities from the "Activities" section of this chapter. Ask your student to try an activity or two, and talk with her about how she is feeling about the task. If she appears truly not to be enjoying the work, help her finish quickly and go on to another writing project. If other students in a group are working on stories, it's often best to let this student work on a research report.

The second group—the most common among students with special needs—is the one in which students want to write stories, but don't really know how. If asked to write a story, for example, about an animal who is in danger, they have difficulty thinking about what animal to write about. If they're able to get started, they frequently don't like their opening, and then they don't know what to say next. Generally, they feel overwhelmed. We see them sitting with their papers and pencils, staring blankly into space. When asked if they want some help, they say, "No, I'm thinking."

Sometimes, they really are thinking. Students in this second group, however, tend not to accomplish much writing. They end the work period feeling unfulfilled and unsuccessful. They haven't gotten much accomplished, and they don't feel good about it.

The most effective way to help these students is to offer activities that are well within their writing capabilities. It's crucial that the writing experiences be pleasurable. Students need to be having fun with their imaginations. Their sense of humor and their love of mystery and adventure can be tapped to help them get excited about their work.

Several favorite activities in this chapter offer a wide range of possibilities for students who are working at all levels, from word to paragraph writing, and beyond.

Students in the third group can, with some encouragement and stimulation, write long stories. They can work independently or with a small amount of support. Sometimes, these students even come to class with their own story ideas.

Provide the time and quiet space for these students to work. Let them write. As long as they are working and feeling satisfied with their work, do not interfere with their natural progress.

You can offer suggestions on character development, plot, or the setting, but do it sparingly and with great care. Many writers report that they feel stifled if people comment on their work before it is completed. They like to be alone with their work until they feel ready to share.

Students will vary greatly in their reactions to comments on their stories— even positive comments. The most important thing you can do is watch. If students are engaged with their work, it's probably best to let them work independently.

If you have a student who is advanced with story writing, and who wants help and critique in developing this skill, there are books that teach how to write fiction. A favorite is *In Your Own Words, a Beginner's Guide to Writing*, revised ed., by Sylvia Cassedy (Harper and Row, 1990). This book has wonderful information on many types and aspects of story writing, such as plot, character development, and writing good dialogue. It also has sections on other forms of writing, such as letters and poetry.

Encourage students who are capable and enthusiastic story writers to gain experience also in nonfiction. They will need the latter skill as they progress through school.

A NOTE ON SHARING

Students can enjoy reading their creative writing to each other. As with all sharing, however, this must be optional, because some students are shy about their work. It is particularly helpful if you also read your work during sharing times, because this provides excellent modeling.

When your students read, ask them if they want feedback on their work. If they say no, they should be thanked for reading their work once they are done, and very general comments, such as "I really enjoyed your story" can be made.

If a person wants feedback, only positive comments should be made. Talk with your students ahead of time about this, and teach them how to give positive feedback. Model comments such as "I liked the way your hero was so brave and ran to get help" or "You did such a good job on the setting that when you were reading, I really believed I was sitting on the shore. I could smell the ocean."

Constructive criticism is helpful for very advanced writers, but when people are starting out, they need to hear what they are doing right. This will encourage their continued writing.

ACTIVITIES

The following 10 activities stimulate story writing. They are favorites.

1. **Illustrate a scene in a story.** Even beginning students can start on the road to writing stories. Help students select favorite books. Ask them to describe scenes they would like to illustrate.

   An alternative is to ask students to think about how their favorite stories ended. Do they think that it's possible for something else to happen to the characters? Would they like to continue the stories with an illustration or two?

   Once the pictures are done, ask students to write each book's title and author on their drawings. They can also write any words that they think are appropriate on their illustrations or on separate sheets of paper.

2. **Answer questions about a story starter.** For this activity, give your students a story starter. Ask them to answer specific questions about the situation being presented.

   This is a good activity for students at all levels. Students working on word writing skills can enjoy answering the questions and drawing a picture to show what happens next. More advanced students can continue on with the story with sentences or paragraphs. Six independent activity sheets, all titled "A Story," illustrate this type of story starter. They are found on pages 92–97.

3. **Write a story when shown a picture.** Here, you provide interesting pictures for your students to write about. Fascinating pictures can be found in newspapers and magazines. It's a good idea to develop a file of them.

   A particularly effective resource to use for pictures is the book *The Mysteries of Harris Burdick* by Chris Van Allsburg (Houghton Mifflin, 1984). This book has a series of fascinating black-and-white drawings, each one of which is accompanied by a title and the first line of a possible story. One of the pictures depicts a house taking off from the ground as if it were a rocket. Another shows a man raising a chair as if to strike a large bump in his rug. Students really enjoy writing stories to these pictures.

4. **Write a serial story.** This is a favorite activity for many students. You need at least two writers, but the activity works best if there are at least three or four people participating.

    Each person starts by writing a one-sentence story opener on the top of a piece of paper. Sentences like "The girl sat by the river" and "He didn't know if he could get there in time" are good openings. Once everyone has finished his or her sentence, the papers are passed to the next person on the right. That person adds to the story.

    There are only two rules:

    • You can never write more than one sentence in a turn.

    • You cannot kill off another person's character.

    Once the story has returned to the person who started it, that person can read it aloud. Then, either a new story can be started or the original can be continued with another round. Sometimes, these stories go on to great lengths.

5. **Write a story when given a story starter.** These story starters are quick little openings that can generate great stories. Use the "Story Starters" on pages 98–100. Copy the pages and cut out whatever story starters are being used. Then, students can keep their openings with them in their folders.

6. **Write a WHO did WHAT story.** First, generate a WHO did WHAT list. With your students, brainstorm a series of at least 15 different characters, such as "a grandmother" and "a boy." If students wish to add more detail, such as "a grandmother in a wheelchair" and "a boy on a rickety bicycle," they can do so. Write each character on a separate index card.

    Next, brainstorm a series of incidents, such as "goes on a trip" and "robs a bank." Write each of these on its own index card, also.

    Shuffle the cards and place them face down on the table in two separate piles. Students select a character card (a WHO) and an incident card (a WHAT). They then have to write a story using them. Some very humorous WHO did WHAT stories can emerge, and students enjoy the challenge.

7. **Write a FIVE-OBJECT FIND story.** For this activity, ask your students to select some objects from the room. Get no more than ten of these and place them on the table.

    Students then mentally select five of the objects. They write the names of the objects on a piece of paper. You then provide a story situation into which they will weave the five objects. Four "Five-Object Find" activity sheets are provided on pages 101–104.

Once students are used to this kind of story, they often like to bring objects from home. The key is that they don't know what the story will involve until after the objects are selected.

8. **Write a very long excuse.** This is a most enjoyable activity that focuses on humor. A person acknowledges that she's made a mistake, but then she writes a lengthy story that is a good explanation for the transgression. For example, if she's agreed that she has, in fact, not taken out the trash, she can describe in great detail the other important crises that have prevented her from fulfilling this responsibility: her broken fingernail, for example.

   Three pages of transgressions, "A Very Long Excuse—Story Starters," are offered on pages 105–107. Copy the pages and then give individual students copies of whatever excuses they are working on.

9. **Write a THIS IS HOW I . . . story.** For this activity, provide a series of stimulus sentences. They can fall in the realistic genre, such as "This is how I saved my little sister." They can also be humorous, such as "This is how I ate one hundred pizzas." For the humorous stories, students often like to show how an illogical exaggeration can have a perfectly logical explanation. For example, for the pizza incident, they could start with "Well, you see, I was making miniature pizzas one afternoon and . . ."

   Two pages of "This Is How I . . . Story Starters" are provided on pages 108–109. Copy these pages and then give individual students copies of whatever "This is how I . . ." sentences they are working on.

10. **Write a HELP! THERE'S AN . . . ABC story.** This activity is done in a group. It's even possible for different groups to work on it throughout the school day to create a good story.

    First write, "Help! There's an" on the top of a piece of paper. Then write the alphabet, one letter per line, down the page. Then, start a story, using the letters of the alphabet to provide some inspiration.

    For example, this is the start of one such story:

Help! There's an
Alligator who is
Becoming a problem because he is
Coming this way and I
Don't know if he is friendly.
Even if he is (and so on).

    Some students do like to do these stories individually, and they can use the "Help! There's an . . . ABC Story" activity sheet on pages 110–111.

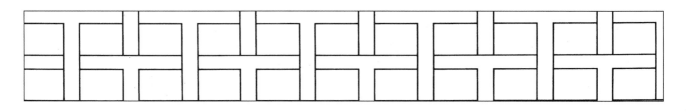

A Story (1)

You are in a submarine doing scientific research in the deepest part of the ocean. You are looking out into the water when, suddenly, you see a bright light and a door. The door opens, and you go through it.

What is the first thing you see? _____

Write some words to describe what you see. _____

_____

How do you feel? _____

Do you go forward, or do you try to go back through the door? _____

_____

Are you still alone? _____

_____

Draw a picture that shows what happens next.

Name _____ **Date** _____

A Story (2)

"Give me your money," the boy says.
"No," you answer. You stare back at him.

What does the boy look like? Write a few words to describe him. _____

_____

What do you look like? Write a few words to describe yourself. _____

_____

Where are you standing? _____

What time of day is it? _____

Are there other people nearby? _____

Does the boy walk away? _____

Draw a picture that shows what happens next.

Name _____ **Date** _____

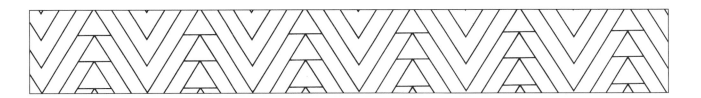

A Story (3)

You are skiing on a mountain. All of a sudden, you see huge footprints in the snow. You follow them into a clump of trees. You see a creature.

How big is the creature? _____

What color is it? _____

What does it look like? Write a few words to describe it. _____

_____

Does it come toward you? _____

Do you talk to it? _____

What do you say? _____

Does the creature have friends in nearby clumps of trees? _____

Draw a picture that shows what happens next.

Name _____   **Date** _____

A Story (4)

You have been alone on the ocean in your canoe for several days. Finally, you spot an island off to the east. As you approach, you see a man waving frantically to you.

What does the man look like? Write a few words to describe him. _____

_____

What does the island look like? Write a few words to describe the island.

_____

_____

Is the man yelling to you? _____

Can you hear any words? If so, what is he yelling? _____

_____

Do you paddle toward the man? _____

Draw a picture that shows what happens next.

Name _____ **Date** _____

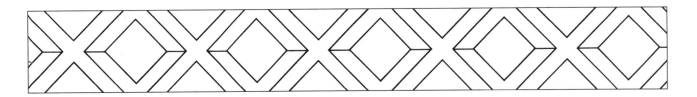

A Story (5)

You are a mouse who lives in an abandoned building. One morning, you hear beautiful music coming from the basement. When you go to investigate, you see no one there. The music is coming from the center of the empty room.

What does the music sound like? Write a few words to describe it. _____

_____

What does the basement look like? Write a few words to describe it. _____

_____

How do you feel? _____

Do you look further for the source of the music? _____

Do you hear other sounds? If so, write a few words to describe them. _____

_____

Draw a picture that shows what happens next.

Name _____   **Date** _____

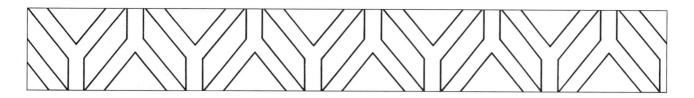

A Story (6)

You are visiting the circus when, suddenly, a woman walks up to you. "Quick," she says. "Put this on. We're due in the big tent in five minutes." She is holding out a clown costume.

You put the costume on over your clothes and follow the woman to the center of the ring.

How many clowns are already there? _____

How many people are in the audience? _____

What does your clown costume look like? Write a few words to describe it.

_____

How do you feel? _____

What are the other clowns doing? Write a few words to describe their actions.

_____

Do you join in with what the other clowns are doing? _____

Draw a picture that shows what happens next.

Name _____ **Date** _____

Story Starters

__ __ __ __ __ __ __ __ __ __ __ __ __ __ __ __ __

I am a green monster, and at the moment, I am very hungry.

__ __ __ __ __ __ __ __ __ __ __ __ __ __ __ __ __

It was true. The elephant was following me.

__ __ __ __ __ __ __ __ __ __ __ __ __ __ __ __ __

My mother was not going to be pleased. There was a six-foot snake in our bathtub.

__ __ __ __ __ __ __ __ __ __ __ __ __ __ __ __ __

I stared at my hands. There were red dots all over them.

__ __ __ __ __ __ __ __ __ __ __ __ __ __ __ __ __

José jumped. Then he remembered. His parachute was still in the airplane.

__ __ __ __ __ __ __ __ __ __ __ __ __ __ __ __ __

David felt in his pocket. Oh no! His money was gone.

__ __ __ __ __ __ __ __ __ __ __ __ __ __ __ __ __

Keesha raced toward the pond. She yelled to him. She had to save him.

__ __ __ __ __ __ __ __ __ __ __ __ __ __ __ __ __

Patrick covered his ears. The wind was so loud. Would the barn hold?

__ __ __ __ __ __ __ __ __ __ __ __ __ __ __ __ __

Sophia felt the sharp pain as she landed. Now, how was she going to get home?

__ __ __ __ __ __ __ __ __ __ __ __ __ __ __ __ __

Jared woke to the sound of the train whistle. He looked outside. They were traveling through a city. But where were the people? Come to think of it, where were the other passengers on the train?

__ __ __ __ __ __ __ __ __ __ __ __ __ __ __ __ __

She meant to travel back to 1860. But the time machine must have needed a little adjustment. Because there she was, standing in the shadow of a brontosaurus.

__ __ __ __ __ __ __ __ __ __ __ __ __ __ __ __ __

Story Starters (continued)

————————————————————————————————

Eric stared at the spider's web. He gasped. It looked as if the tiny creature caught within was holding up a sign.

————————————————————————————————

Mary kicked the locked door. When was her mom going to get home?

————————————————————————————————

"Can't you drive faster?" Jackson asked. He cradled the sick puppy in his arms.

————————————————————————————————

Elena watched the shore fade from view. She really was doing it. She was sailing the Atlantic Ocean to Africa.

————————————————————————————————

He looked like a run-of-the-mill, normal gorilla when he walked into town. But little did the people know that life would never be the same.

————————————————————————————————

Carlos made himself breathe. He knew he was ready. The 100-meter dash was his best race.

————————————————————————————————

The sound started at 3 A.M. Blop. Blop. Joan got out of bed to investigate.

————————————————————————————————

"Over here," the photographers yelled. "Over here."

————————————————————————————————

Isaac ran to the house. When were they going to leave him alone?

————————————————————————————————

The teacher seemed normal that morning. But then, right before math, she started to shrink.

————————————————————————————————

He found the ring on the top of the truck.

————————————————————————————————

"I thought I wanted to get married," Bruce said. "But now, I don't know."

————————————————————————————————

"I have a twin sister?" Carlotta asked.

————————————————————————————————

Story Starters (continued)

— —

It was narrow, too narrow to get through. There must be another way out of this cave.

— —

"I didn't steal it," Helen said. She looked away.

— —

The mud oozed up past her ankles. Still, she kept on the path, following the dog.

— —

Victor lifted the kitten out of the trash can. The kitten shivered, then purred.

— —

Nicole tightened her grip on the bat. She had to hit the next one. The count was 3 and 2.

— —

"Well, look at that," Michael said. He stopped the tractor next to the baby doe.

— —

When Donna told him he was covered with pimples, he thought she was kidding. Then, he looked at himself in the mirror.

— —

The key fit. Jesse entered the attic. Now she would find out why Aunt Kathryn had kept it closed for so long.

— —

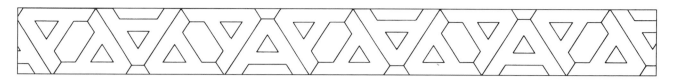

Five-Object Find (1)

You are hiding in a deserted cave. You entered the cave with nothing, but in a corner, you find the following objects:

1. _____
2. _____
3. _____
4. _____
5. _____

    You hear noises outside. What do you do? How will you use the five objects to help yourself?

Start your story here.

_____

_____

_____

_____

_____

_____

_____

_____

_____

_____

_____

_____

Name _____   **Date** _____

Five-Object Find (2)

You are walking in the park one afternoon when you see a large box in the middle of the path. You look in and find:

1. _____

2. _____

3. _____

4. _____

5. _____

    When you take the objects out, you become dizzy and faint. You wake up in an empty room. The objects are lying on a table.

    How do you use the objects to escape from the room and find out what happened?

Start your story here.

_____

_____

_____

_____

_____

_____

_____

_____

_____

_____

Name _____ **Date** _____

Five-Object Find (3)

You are lost in a forest. You have only your clothes and a strong will to go home. You stumble upon an empty cabin in the middle of a clearing. In the cabin, you find:

1. _____

2. _____

3. _____

4. _____

5. _____

How do you use these things to find your way home?

Start your story here.

_____

_____

_____

_____

_____

_____

_____

_____

_____

_____

_____

_____

Name _____ **Date** _____

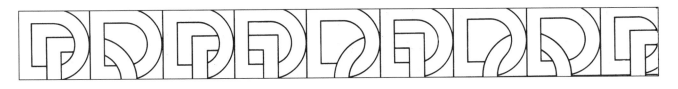

Five-Object Find (4)

You are in an elevator in a huge office building, going up to the fourth floor. The elevator stops short, and the door opens. You find yourself in a long, empty corridor with no doors or windows. On the floor, you find:

1. _____

2. _____

3. _____

4. _____

5. _____

    How do you use these objects to get to the fourth floor?

Start your story here.

_____

_____

_____

_____

_____

_____

_____

_____

_____

_____

_____

_____

Name _____ **Date** _____

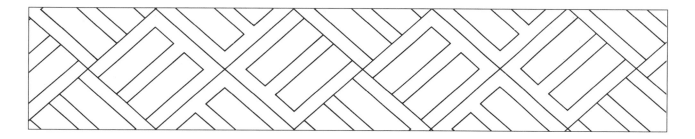

A Very Long Excuse—Story Starters

— —

This is why I was late.

— —

This is why I didn't do my homework.

— —

This is why I ate the whole chocolate cake.

— —

This is why I spent your twenty dollars.

— —

This is why I roller-bladed in the grocery store.

— —

This is why I told my little sister I was Bigfoot.

— —

This is why I forgot to send you a birthday card.

— —

This is why I wasn't here yesterday.

— —

This is why I wore my motorcycle helmet to math class.

— —

This is why I dyed my hair purple and orange.

— —

A Very Long Excuse (continued)

— —

This is why I missed the bus.

— —

This is why I can't do the dishes.

— —

This is why I didn't take out the trash.

— —

This is why I can't eat even a bite of broccoli.

— —

This is why I can't let anyone see my science project. Ever.

— —

This is why I was standing on top of the art table when the teacher came into the room.

— —

This is why I pretended to be sick.

— —

This is why I didn't have time to feed the cat.

— —

This is why I broke our date last Friday.

— —

This is why I just had to sit on your plate of spaghetti.

— —

This is why I dug up your flower garden.

— —

This is why I lost my keys, my wallet, and my shoes.

— —

This is why I can't wear a hat in the winter, even when it's ten degrees below zero.

This is why I can't go to sleep so early.

This is why I just have to watch TV for the rest of the school year.

This is why I had to go to the movies instead of mowing the lawn.

This is why I missed basketball practice.

This is why I can't take the part of the talking turtle in the school play.

This is why I didn't study for the history test.

This is why I let my ten-year-old sister give me a haircut.

This is why I forgot to show up at my own birthday party.

This is why I charged my new sweater to your VISA card.

This is why I called the newspaper and told them I saw five aliens at the laundromat.

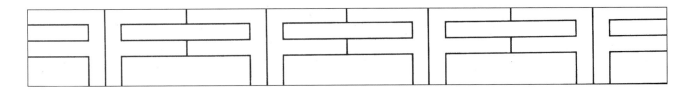

This Is How I . . . Story Starters

_ _

This is how I annoyed my older brother last Wednesday.

_ _

This is how I escaped from the Martians.

_ _

This is how I rescued the moose who was wandering in our neighborhood.

_ _

This is how I won the basketball game, and I was only in the game for two minutes.

_ _

This is how I saved my sister.

_ _

This is how I found the treasure.

_ _

This is how I ate one hundred pizzas.

_ _

This is how I got out of doing homework all last year.

_ _

This is how I got rid of my pimples.

_ _

This is how I started my world-famous heavy metal band.

_ _

This is how I traveled to China.

_ _

This is how I captured the Loch Ness monster.

_ _

This is how I survived the hurricane.

_ _

This is how I saved my best friend's reputation.

_ _

This is how I found my way back through the forest.

_ _

This Is How I . . . (continued)

— —

This is how I got a ride in the spaceship.

— —

This is how I jumped over the high school.

— —

This is how I caught a one-hundred-pound trout. Honest.

— —

This is how I met Abraham Lincoln (or any famous historical or contemporary person).

— —

This is how I found the very bottom of the Pacific Ocean (or any fantasy place).

— —

This is how I found Cinderella's slipper (or any other cartoon character's prop).

— —

This is how I avoided the fight with the school bully.

— —

This is how I kept my parents from getting divorced.

— —

This is how I learned to drive a car.

— —

This is how I got my job at the herring factory.

— —

This is how I figured out that I could fly faster than a speeding bullet, just like Superman.

— —

This is how I stopped the earthquake.

— —

This is how I forgot my own name.

— —

This is how I became merged with my computer.

— —

This is how I rescued fourteen people from the fire.

— —

This is how I hit the baseball over the fence all the way to the outskirts of the city.

— —

Help! There's an . . . ABC Story

For this story, you will get some help—the use of the alphabet. Write a story that follows the format like that shown here:

HELP! THERE'S AN

Amazing termite who is

Bigger than a baseball, and he is

Chewing my desk. I

Doubt if the

Exterminators will . . . (and so on).

Try an ABC story here.

HELP! THERE'S AN

A _____

B _____

C _____

D _____

E _____

F _____

G _____

H _____

I _____

J _____

Help! There's an . . . (continued)

K _____

L _____

M _____

N _____

O _____

P _____

Q _____

R _____

S _____

T _____

U _____

V _____

W _____

X _____

Y _____

Z _____

Name _____   **Date** _____

WRITING ESSAYS

Essays provide excellent writing experience for advanced students who are comfortable with paragraph writing. For a discussion of paragraph writing, including the use of a structured five-sentence paragraph that has a topic sentence, three supporting detail sentences, and an ending sentence, please refer to the "Paragraph Writing" chapter of this book, page 38.

To be successful in junior high school, high school, and college, students will be expected to write answers to essay questions. They will also be asked to express their opinions and to demonstrate their knowledge in many other written forms.

These expectations are not the only reasons, however, for essay writing. Short essays provide students with the opportunity to write a lot. Through this extensive practice, they gain the feeling that writing is like talking. If they have opinions and ideas they can tell a friend, then they can also write down these thoughts on a piece of paper. They become able to write on a wide variety of topics, and they are able to approach most writing tasks with confidence.

It is a challenge, however, to begin this work. Up to this point, a great deal of structure has been provided. Often, students need encouragement to begin this freer essay form.

Use the following technique for teaching beginning essay writing. This work can be done with one student or, ideally, with a small group of up to six students.

1. **Brainstorm a series of topics that you and your students know a lot about.** These topics can fall in the following areas:

   - Subjects that you will present information about, such as rock groups and transportation.
   - Opinion statements about political issues.
   - Opinion statements about personal and moral issues.

     Record all suggested topics. Three topic sheets—one for each type of topic—are provided on pages 114–116. Students can refer to them if they are having trouble thinking of ideas. Often, this happens at the early stages of the essay writing work. Once students are comfortable with the form, they tend to be enthusiastic in their suggestions as to what to write about.

2. **Once you have a good list of possible topics, read the list aloud to your students. Then, allow each person to select one topic in turn.** If you are working with one student, alternate choices between the two of you. If you are working with a group and there is good-natured controversy as to who gets to choose first, have everyone roll a die to determine the sequence of selectors.

3. **The person who is first chooses a topic. Then, everyone in the group writes freely about it for ten minutes.** When you are starting out, students can be nervous about this. They worry that they won't say things right or that they'll make mistakes. They may tell you that they don't know enough about a subject to write about it.

   If students continue to be insecure, even if they are given support, tell them that you are going to show them how to write about something that they know absolutely nothing about by doing this yourself. For example, you could tell them that you are a basketball fan, but that you know nothing about football. You'll choose for your topic: Famous Football Players.

   As you write, read aloud what you are doing. For this subject, you could write:

   > There are many famous football players. They are big. Very big. I'm sure that they are quite a bit larger than anyone in this room.
   >   I also think that famous football players probably have to be fast. They have to keep running after one another. They also have to keep running after that ball that they all chase.

   It helps to put humor in your model. Laughter and silliness can help take away the fear of failure. Your goal at this stage is not to have students write serious, well-structured essays. They will develop the ability to do so in time. At this point, the main goal is to help them write freely.

4. **Once everyone has written for ten minutes, ask people to share their work.** If a student is reluctant to do so, allow her this privacy. It is good, however, to encourage students to read their work as much as possible. It helps students to hear how other writers have handled a particular topic, so group work is especially beneficial for the essay form.

   If a student is repeatedly reluctant to share, tell him at the beginning of the next essay writing session that you will be asking to read his work silently at the end of class. Once you have done so, point out positive aspects of his work. Doing this several times often helps him to develop the confidence to share.

5. **For the next essay writing session, the second person chooses the topic, and so on.** The practice and the lightheartedness with which this work is approached are the keys to success.

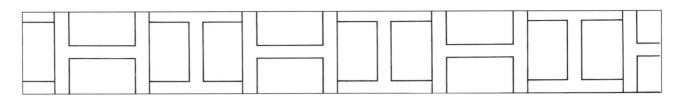

"Write About" Topics for Short Essays

1. any famous living person
2. any historical person
3. any politician
4. any famous event
5. any singer
6. any actor or actress
7. any artist
8. any sports figure
9. any musician
10. any scientist
11. any poet
12. any writer
13. any hero or heroine
14. any villain
15. any musical group
16. any cartoon character
17. any country
18. any state
19. any city
20. any natural wonder
21. any man-made wonder
22. any planet
23. any river or lake
24. any flower
25. any tree
26. any plant
27. any food
28. any animal
29. any endangered species
30. any weather
31. any natural phenomenon
32. any mode of transportation
33. any invention
34. any sport
35. any job
36. any condition that imposes a challenge
37. any song
38. any book
39. any book character
40. any movie

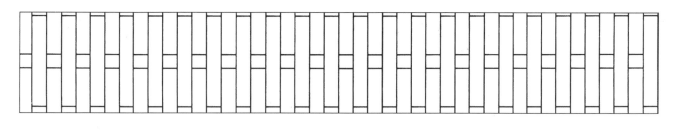

Political Topics for Short Essays

1. Is there too much violence on TV?

2. Should a college education be free to all students?

3. Should research testing on animals be allowed?

4. Do people in inner cities have the same chances for advancement as people in the suburbs?

5. Should cigarettes become illegal?

6. Should more money be spent to fight pollution?

7. Is it important to vote?

8. Should marijuana be legalized?

9. Should censorship of books, movies, and TV shows be encouraged to protect young people?

10. Should free homes be provided for homeless people?

11. Should all people who need it be given free food?

12. What is the best way to battle crime?

13. Should jails be places for punishment or rehabilitation?

14. Should sports heroes make as much money as they do?

15. How can people of different races learn to get along better with one another?

16. Do you think that inner cities are a good place to live?

17. Should people be forced to wear seat belts?

18. What do you think should happen to drunk drivers?

19. What do you think the government should spend most of its money on?

20. What do you think about capital punishment?

Personal and Moral Topics for Short Essays

1. What would you do if a friend who is having trouble with a school subject asked you to cheat?

2. Do you think it is ever a good idea to tell a lie?

3. How do you think a person should deal with a bully?

4. What do you think about a teacher who is not respectful to students?

5. What would you say to a friend who is anorexic?

6. What would you do if you were in a car with your best friend, and he or she was driving too fast?

7. Do you think that being rich could make you happy?

8. What would you do if you had a disagreement with someone you didn't know very well?

9. What would you do if you had a disagreement with your best friend?

10. What would you say to a friend if he or she made a racial slur?

11. Would you feel comfortable dating a person of a different race?

12. If you found out someone you know is homeless, what would you do?

13. Do you think there is any difference in areas of talent between males and females?

14. What would you do if you were being discriminated against?

15. If you discovered that a good friend was selling drugs, would you tell anyone about it?

PART TWO

Grammar 119

Editing 133

Writing Poetry 141

The Literature Connection. . . 161

Holidays. 174

Writing Letters 186

Using the Newspaper. 200

Integrating Writing With
   Real Life and the Rest of
   the Curriculum 211

Gimmicks and Gags 219

GRAMMAR

Grammar is the study of the structure of the language. When approached well, this study can facilitate the development of a person's writing skills. The focus must be on how interesting the English language is, and how satisfying it can be to look at the patterns and structures within it.

This study does not have to be extensive at the level at which students are working. Very advanced and professional writers must know specific and detailed grammar rules. Students working with *Let's Write!* however, primarily need to relax with their writing. They need to be comfortable with saying what they think in written language. At this stage, therefore, the main purpose of teaching some grammar is to help students feel more comfortable with the language. This study shows them that the language is not a confused mass of overwhelming details. There are capitalization and punctuation patterns. There are kinds of words that follow systems. If they learn about these patterns, they can understand a little more about how the language is put together.

WHICH GRAMMAR CONCEPTS SHOULD BE TAUGHT, AND WHEN SHOULD THEY BE PRESENTED?

The eight main parts of speech are taught, as well as the concepts of subject and predicate. The basic capitalization and punctuation rules are also presented, including the use of quotation marks.

Approach the grammar study in the following order.

1. **A noun is a person, place, or thing.** This work can begin early, at the Word Writing stage. Advanced students can study nouns that are abstract concepts, such as "originality" and "fear."

2. **A verb is an action word.** This study can be started at the Word Writing stage. Advanced students can look at verbs that are passive action words, such as "believe" and "was."

3. **A sentence consists of a subject (who or what the sentence is about) and a predicate (which tells what is happening, or gives information about the subject).** Every sentence must contain a subject and a predicate, except

for a few one-word statements like "Ouch!" or "Help!" or "Hi!" This study can begin at the Sentence Writing stage.

It is sometimes confusing to students to study nouns and verbs, and then to study subjects and predicates. Most students at first don't understand the difference between nouns and subjects. "Aren't nouns always the subjects?" they ask. "And don't subjects always come at the beginnings of sentences?" The answers are complex. Sometimes, pronouns are subjects. Or in a sentence like "There was a strong wind blowing," the subject is in the middle. In a sentence like "The girl paddled her canoe across the lake," there are several nouns, but only one subject.

Students are more likely to understand these concepts if you talk about the complexities but don't focus on them. Focus instead on the purposes of subjects and predicates. You are looking primarily at the structure of sentences here, not at parts of speech. It particularly helps some students if you present sentences like the one mentioned above, which contain several nouns but only one subject. This helps them understand the purpose of a subject.

This work is very important because many students have either incomplete or run-on sentences in their writing. This study helps them recognize and correct these errors.

4. **Every sentence begins with a capital letter.** This work is begun at the Sentence Writing level.

5. **Every sentence ends with a punctuation mark.** The first two that are presented at the Sentence Writing level are periods and question marks. Exclamation marks can be introduced when you feel that your students are ready to learn them.

6. **An adjective is a word that describes a noun.** This work can be started at the Paragraph Writing level.

7. **An adverb is a word that describes a verb.** This study can be begun at the Paragraph Writing level.

8. **There are words called pronouns, conjunctions, prepositions, and articles in the English language.** Introduce these concepts as a group. Each one should be presented separately, with ample time for instructions, but it's best to let students know that they will be studying a group. Once they have learned about this group, they will be familiar with the main parts of speech in English. This work should be done once your students are comfortable with writing paragraphs.

   The following four parts of speech are being presented:

   • A pronoun is a word that can represent a noun. Common pronouns are <u>she</u>, <u>it</u>, <u>him</u>, and <u>they</u>.

- A conjunction is a joining word. It brings parts of a sentence together. Common conjunctions are <u>because,</u> <u>so,</u> and <u>and.</u>

- A preposition often tells the direction of things. Common prepositions are <u>to,</u> <u>around,</u> and <u>under.</u> A preposition can also tell the relationship of words to each other. Words like <u>with</u> and <u>of</u> serve this purpose.

- An article is a connecting word. The three articles in English are <u>the,</u> <u>a,</u> and <u>an.</u>

9. **Quotation marks are used to separate spoken language from the rest of a sentence.** This work should be done when students are comfortable with paragraph writing. If students are writing dialogue at the sentence writing and beginning paragraph writing levels, you can show them how to use quotation marks, but do not hold them accountable for this knowledge. At those stages, approach it as something interesting to see.

10. **There are seven important places where you capitalize the first letter in a word.** They are the following:

- the first word of a sentence

- specific names of people, places, and organizations

- the word "I"

- names of groups of people, including religions, and also deities such as "God," "Allah," and "Buddha"

- all the important words in titles

- the first word of a quotation

- all dates, including days of the week

It usually works best to teach these rules as a unit, while providing enough time for students to become familiar with each one. The goal is for students to begin noticing capitalization in their reading, and for them to carry this new knowledge into their writing.

This work should start when students are comfortable with paragraph writing. Even though students have already studied the first rule, which is to capitalize the first words in sentences, and they are probably familiar with the next two, it's best to approach this work as a study of capitalization in general. It helps students to list all the important rules.

11. **Commas help represent a pause in spoken English.** They help avoid confusion in written language. There are four important places to use commas:

- Before a conjunction in the middle of a sentence, when the conjunction separates two smaller sentences. (It was a rainy day, so Elena went back and got her umbrella.)

- Between items that are listed in a sentence, including before a conjunction in a series. (Adam asked for a pad of paper, a pencil, a set of water colors, and an easel for his birthday.)

- To separate a quotation from the rest of the sentence. ("Please help me lift this table," Marcus said. Aaron asked, "Are you busy this weekend?")

- To help avoid confusion. (To Patty, Martha was a friend.)

There are many more comma rules. Rather than present all of them, however, it's good to study these few common and important ones. By mastering a few, students gain the feeling that there is a structure to punctuation. If they wish to study other rules, there are many grammar books that provide information about them. This work should start only when students are very comfortable with writing paragraphs.

HOW TO TEACH GRAMMAR CONCEPTS AND USAGE

Introduce grammar concepts in a relaxed and straightforward manner. For example, if students are beginning the study of nouns, you can say, "Today, we're going to look at words that represent people, places, and things. These words are called nouns."

Concepts should be presented as concretely as possible. For example, when nouns are being introduced, it's helpful to bring in some objects, such as an arrowhead, a fossil, a bar of soap, and a walnut. Pictures of places and people can be shown.

It's critically important to present only one concept at a time and to reinforce this learning extensively. Review is also very important.

Students with special needs learn grammar best, and—most important—they retain this knowledge when their study is reinforced and reviewed with interactive activities. Games are very effective. It is also good to use a student's own writing to look at grammar concepts.

ACTIVITIES

All the activities listed below are interactive in nature; worksheets do not seem to be effective tools for students with special needs to learn grammar. Students can successfully complete worksheets, but whatever knowledge they gain does not seem to carry over into their writing.

1. **Play the "Noun" game.** Students make a pack of at least forty cards by writing one noun per card. Standard 3″ × 5″ index cards work well for this

purpose. The cards are placed face down on the table. Depending on the level of your students, you can ask them to pick up one, two, or three cards. Once they have picked up their nouns, their job is to make up a good sentence using them. If they are successful, they keep the cards. The player with the most cards at the end wins the game. As with writing tasks, you are always a player in this game, to provide good modeling for sentences.

For advanced students, players can roll a die. Once they roll a number from one to six, they then pick up that many nouns and attempt to make up a good sentence with them. Students greatly enjoy this game.

2. **Play the "Verb" game.** This game is played in the same manner as the noun game—the difference being that verbs are used instead of nouns. Verb endings and tenses can be changed as needed. It's best not to use more than three verbs.

3. **Play the "Subject and Predicate" game.** Once students are familiar with the concepts of subject and predicate, they make up a deck of cards for this game, again using 3″ × 5″ index cards. For every pair of cards, they write the subject of a sentence on one, for example, "The cat"; and a predicate on the other, for example, "ran up a tree." A large "S" is written on the back side of the subject cards, and a large "P" is written on the back side of the predicate cards.

Once the deck is prepared, all cards are placed face down on the table in random order. Students select one subject and one predicate. If the resulting sentence makes sense, they keep the cards. If not, they have to return them to the table in the same place. At the end, the player with the most cards wins the game.

Sometimes, students enjoy trying to convince their peers that a sentence does in fact make sense. For example, if the subject and predicate combine to say, "The dog flew the airplane," they might argue, "Well, it was a really smart dog, and his owner became suddenly sick while she was flying and she couldn't use her arms. So the pilot told her dog how to steer with his mouth, and she told him what buttons to press with his nose. So he helped fly the plane." This is a great verbalization activity, and it's also fun.

4. **Have a contest to see who can write the most nouns.** An example of some good contest rules are offered on page 127, "Write the Most Nouns Contest Rules."

Many students enjoy competing with one another. For those who do not, you can vary the contest by having every person who writes more than fifty nouns declared a winner. Some groups prefer to see how many nouns they can write cooperatively as a team.

This activity can also be used with verbs, adjectives, and adverbs.

5. **Play "Verb Charades."** With your students, brainstorm a group of approximately sixteen verbs that you record on index cards, one per card. Divide students into teams, and have each team choose an actor. One of the actors secretly chooses a card and then acts it out for his or her team. If the team calls out the correct verb within one minute, they get a point, and the next team tries to discover their verb. The team with the most points at the end wins the game.

6. **Play the "Category" game with parts of speech.** Provide an interesting object or picture, and then brainstorm with your students some nouns and verbs that relate to the stimulus. For instance, if you bring in a football, your nouns could be "team," "player," "San Francisco 49ers," "football," "helmet," and so on. Your verbs could be, "kick," "run," "pass," "throw," "punt," and so on. Record these words on a piece of paper or on the chalkboard.

   This game can be varied to accommodate many levels. For students who are just beginning, record each word on an index card, and provide written labels for the categories "Nouns" and "Verbs." Then together, place each card into its proper category.

   More advanced students can write the words themselves on a piece of paper. An example of a more advanced game, "Where Does the Word Belong?" is shown on page 128.

   This game of categories can be used at all levels for all parts of speech. It's best not to use more than three categories at one time.

7. **Play the "Quick Sort" game.** This is a variation of the category game, but it has an added element of speed. You will need a stopwatch for this game.

   Decide on two or three categories of parts of speech with which you will work. For example, you might decide to work with verbs and adverbs. Make labels for the separate piles.

   With your students, brainstorm a list of at least forty words. Make sure that there are several representatives of each type of word when they are sorted. Record each word on an index card.

   Shuffle the deck and hand it to the first player. Time him as he sorts the cards into their appropriate piles as quickly as he can. The next player then gets a turn. Players can try to beat their own time, or they can be competitive with one another.

8. **Play the "Word Blind" game.** For this game, tell your students that they will be filling in the blanks in some sentences, but that there is a slight problem: They will not know in advance the sentences they will be completing. Have each student write a list of ten nouns. Then, read them ten sentences that you have prepared in advance, each of which has a missing

noun. Students then complete the sentences with their nouns, in the order in which they have written them.

The resulting sentences can be quite amusing, and students love this sometimes very humorous activity. An activity sheet with ten sentences with missing nouns, "Finish These Sentences" is offered on page 129.

This activity also works well with adjectives and adverbs, as well as for verbs, as long as the verbs are kept in the past tense and the sentences are chosen with care. Use the "Finish These Sentences" page, with ten sentences that are missing verbs, on page 130.

9. **Play the "Search and Destroy" game.** In this game, you provide some text. Tell your students that they are going to discover if nouns (or any other part of speech you are working with) are important. Without this part of speech, would people still be able to understand what was being communicated?

Give a copy of the text to each student. Tell them to find all the nouns (or other type or word) and cross them all out. Assist your students in finding them all. Then, have someone read the text without the crossed-out words, and see if meaning is impaired. You can use the "Search and Destroy" example on page 131 or make up your own text.

10. **Play the "Try to Find the Meaning" game.** Prepare text in advance. This writing should be of paragraph length, and should contain no beginning capitalization or ending punctuation. An example of three such paragraphs, "Can You Read This?" is provided on page 132.

Give a copy of the text to each student. Then, together, see if you can figure out what the writer meant to say. This graphic example of how necessary beginning capitalization and ending punctuation are often helps students remember to include them in their own writing.

11. **Play the "What Is Each Word?" game.** This game is appropriate once students have studied all eight main parts of speech. For this activity, everyone first writes one sentence. Then they switch papers, so that people are working with someone else's sentence. Students must label every word in the sentence as to the type of word it is. If there is confusion, they can discuss the issue and make their best guess.

The purpose of this activity is not to be absolutely accurate in terms of exact names of parts of speech. It is, rather, to help students discover that all words serve particular functions and often follow regular patterns in their usage.

12. **Play the "Let's Talk" game.** This activity helps students understand the purpose of quotation marks. Begin by modeling. Tell your students something like "I saw a black squirrel this morning." Write down the sentence you have just said either on the chalkboard or on a large piece of paper. Draw a

large circle around it. Then, add the proper quotation marks, and erase the circle. Add the proper "I said."

Next, ask one of your students to tell the group something in a simple sentence. Repeat the recording, drawing the circle, and then finally adding the quotation marks with the proper speaker identification. This activity particularly helps students to understand how to deal with quotation marks in an interrupted quotation in a sentence.

Write the Most Nouns
Contest Rules

1. All nouns are to be written on lined paper.

2. All students will be able to write ten nouns and only ten nouns in class.

3. All contestants will write more nouns during their free time. All contestants can choose how many nouns they wish to write.

4. The person who writes the most nouns will win first prize. Second and third prizes will also be awarded.

5. Entries are due on (date) _____ at (time) _____ .

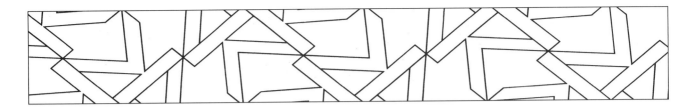

Where Does the Word Belong?

basketball   won

threw   dribbled

player   team

jumped   free throw

walked   sneakers

game   ran

Place the words in their proper categories.

NOUN   **VERB**

_____   _____

_____   _____

_____   _____

_____   _____

_____   _____

_____   _____

Name _____   **Date** _____

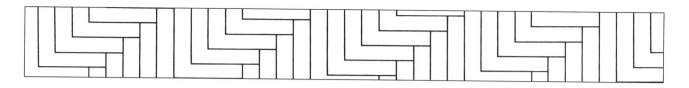

Finish These Sentences

Stop! Do not look at these sentences until you have written a list of ten nouns. Then, take your nouns and put them in the sentences, in the order written. You may not have sentences that always make sense, but you will have fun.

1. The boy kicked the _____ .

2. Sam sat on the _____ and watched TV.

3. The wind howled and the _____ roared.

4. Olga lifted the _____ into the truck.

5. The dog listened carefully to his _____ .

6. Kathy saw a _____ running down the road.

7. The boat sailed off into the _____ .

8. Leroy told _____ that he wanted to go to the movies.

9. Sophia cleaned the _____ and then made supper.

10. Ben put the _____ into the bookshelf.

Name _____   **Date** _____

Finish These Sentences

Stop! Do not look at these sentences until you have written a list of ten verbs. Then, take your verbs and put them in the sentences, in the order written. You may not always have sentences that make sense, but you will have fun.

1. Jelani _____ the whole pizza.

2. The lion _____ the wildlife photographer.

3. Sarah _____ her horse and then went for a ride.

4. Matt _____ the soccer ball once and scored a goal.

5. The rain _____ on the roof.

6. Lian went into the garden and _____ .

7. Abdul put the jump rope down and _____ .

8. The two friends _____ the haunted house.

9. The plane _____ on the runway.

10. Beth _____ the flat tire and drove off.

Name _____ **Date** _____

Search and Destroy

Find all the nouns and cross them out. Then, read what you have left and see if it makes any sense.

A boy sat on a bench and watched two squirrels chasing each other up and down a tree. The squirrels were fast, and the boy admired them.

The sunshine and fresh air made the boy relax. He closed his eyes and listened to the squirrels who were chattering.

Soon, the boy realized that he was hungry. He took a candy bar out of his pocket and began to eat it. Then, he put the wrapper back in his pocket, got off the bench, and went home.

The squirrels sat together in the tree and watched the boy walk away. Then, the animals went back to chasing each other.

Name _____   **Date** _____

Can You Read This?

Try to figure out where the ending punctuation marks should be in the following paragraphs. Then, capitalize the first letter in every word that begins a sentence.

PARAGRAPH ONE

this is a good day it is sunny out and warm we will be able to go to the park and have a picnic it will be a lot of fun

PARAGRAPH TWO

two women went fishing on a lake they didn't catch anything but they kept trying they fished for two hours with no luck then they each threw their lines in one more time both of them caught a big fish

PARAGRAPH THREE

it started raining the boy ran all the way home he was soaked by the time he reached his front door the boy found his key he smiled as he opened his door

Name _____   **Date** _____

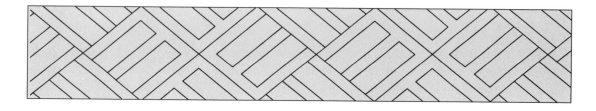

EDITING

The ability to self-edit is an important skill for writers to attain. Unfortunately, this is also an area where students with special needs have often experienced failure and frustration, because of their weaknesses with spelling, the mechanics of language, and organization.

Teachers sometimes take students' writing and then give it back neatly typed, with all of the errors corrected. This is not necessarily a bad thing to do. Often, young children, especially, are highly motivated by seeing their work in such a form. When used sparingly, this technique can assist a person's writing development.

A problem arises, however, when this is the major editing technique employed. Students can begin to feel less ownership of their work because someone else has to "fix it up" before it can be read and enjoyed. Excessive use of this technique can create passivity and discouragement. Feelings like "My writing is so full of mistakes that I'll never be able to get it right," and "I'll always need someone else to help me" can abound.

Worse still, many students have unfortunately had people point out their errors to them. These people can be parents, teachers, or peers. Siblings may have been judgmental and may have harshly pointed out mistakes. However this comes about, most students with writing difficulties seem to be aware at some level that they are not writing in the conventional way.

The goals, therefore, are:

- To help students become accountable for correcting any errors that they are capable of correcting independently.
- To help students become confident self-editors.

Learning self-editing skills should help students feel that they are strong, capable writers who have a lot to say. They will make some errors, as all writers do, but they will be able to find and correct their mistakes. If there are advanced grammar or spelling issues, they will know that they can ask for help.

Two basic principles for teaching these editing skills are:

- Students should be held accountable only for spelling, grammar, and organizational issues that they are capable of recognizing and correcting.

133

- Editing should be learned in a sequential way. A suggested sequence is as follows:

1. Individual words have structural components that make them unique. For example, some words are long, whereas others are short. Some words have endings such as "ed" and "ing." The first letter in a word is an important clue to how it sounds.

    Noticing individual words begins at the Word Writing level.

2. Every sentence begins with a capital letter. This work begins at the Sentence Writing level.

3. Every sentence ends with an ending punctuation mark, such as a period or a question mark. This work begins at the Sentence Writing level.

4. There are conventional ways to spell words. The editing for spelling begins at the Paragraph Writing level and should involve only highly recognizable words. As students progress, they can be held accountable for more advanced spellings.

5. Most sentences, other than one-word sentences like "Hello" or "Ouch" need a subject and a predicate. Incomplete sentences must be recognized and corrected. This work begins at the Paragraph Writing level.

6. Quotation marks are used to separate spoken language from the rest of a sentence. This work begins when students are very comfortable with using quotation marks.

7. There are seven important places where you capitalize the first letter in a word:
   - the first word of a sentence
   - specific names of people, places, and organizations
   - the word "I"
   - names of groups of people, including religions, and also deities such as "God," "Allah," and "Buddha"
   - all the important words in titles
   - the first word of a quotation
   - all dates, including days of the week

    This self-editing work begins when students are very comfortable with all of these rules.

8. Commas help represent a pause in spoken English. They help avoid confusion in written language. There are four important places to use commas:
   - before a conjunction in the middle of a sentence, when the conjunction separates two smaller sentences

- between items that are listed in a sentence, including before a conjunction in a series
- to separate a quotation from the rest of the sentence
- to help avoid confusion

This work begins when students are very comfortable with using all the comma rules.

9. Written work of more than a few sentences should be divided into paragraphs. This makes it easier for the reader to understand the work. The first word in every paragraph must be indented.

    This work can begin once students are comfortable writing texts of at least three paragraphs.

10. Writing should be easily understood, with no confusion for the reader. This work begins when advanced students can hear, with support, any confusing elements in their work.

11. Writing is most easily understood when information and ideas flow with good transitions and organization. This work begins when advanced students can recognize, with support, difficulties with transitions and organization in their work.

12. One point of view must be used consistently in a specific piece of writing. This work begins when advanced students can easily grasp the concept of point of view.

SPECIFIC TECHNIQUES FOR TEACHING SELF-EDITING SKILLS

At the most basic level (item 1 in the sequence), where students are asked to begin to notice written words, ask your student to select a piece of her writing with which she would like to work. Ask her to point out a word that looks interesting. Write the word on a separate sheet of paper and talk about it. If the word is spelled incorrectly, don't point out the errors, but talk about whatever elements are correct. Conduct this discussion in an informal and relaxed manner. If it seems appropriate, select a word or two that you find interesting. Record and discuss these words.

After you have looked at words in general for some time, ask your student to find more specific words. For example, say, "Please find two words in your writing that end with 'ed.'" This beginning editing work can be done in frequent, brief sessions of five minutes or so.

For teaching self-editing at the next level (items 2–8), use a specific technique that has proven effective. First, decide on the elements of spelling, grammar, and organization for which your student can be held accountable. A student could, for example, be held accountable for the following:

- beginning every sentence with a capital letter
- ending every sentence with a period or question mark
- being sure that every sentence (other than one-word exclamatory sentences such as "Wow!") has at least one subject and at least one predicate
- correctly spelling phonetically regular words of one and two syllables
- correctly spelling the phonetically irregular words "the," "was," and "of."

Concerning the last two expectations, you know that this student has a relatively good mastery of spelling phonetically regular words, but that ability to spell irregular words is a problem for him. You have checked work samples, and have discovered that he generally spells the words "the," "was," and "of" correctly.

Sit with your student and together select a short piece of his writing that will be used for this editing work. Ask him to read his work and to look for any capital letters at the beginning of sentences that may be missing. If he finds any, wait while he corrects them.

Next, read his work silently, checking for capitals at the beginning of sentences. If you find any that are missing, put a small pencil checkmark for each one in the margin next to the line where the capital is missing.

Then, ask your student to look at his work again to check for capitals at the beginning of sentences. Tell him that the little pencil marks indicate that he should look especially carefully at those lines, because each check represents a change that needs to be made. When your student has found and corrected his errors, erase the pencil marks. Better still, have him erase them.

Repeat this same procedure with each of the other elements for which your student is being held accountable. The following is a summary of this technique:

1. Ask your student to read her work and to look for one specific type of error.
2. Wait while she corrects any errors she finds.
3. Read the student's work silently and look for the same type of mistake.
4. Put one light pencil checkmark in the margin of each line where an error is found. Put one checkmark for each mistake.
5. Ask your student to read her work again, especially noticing the lines where there are checkmarks. Tell her that each checkmark indicates that a change needs to be made.
6. Once she has discovered her errors, wait while she corrects them.
7. Erase the checkmarks once the errors are corrected.

In the beginning of this work, especially, it is important not to overwhelm students with lots of corrections. Only point out errors that you know your student is capable of seeing and correcting easily. Also, it's a good rule to limit your corrections to five to eight mistakes in a given editing session. The goal is not to have the student produce a perfect work. The goal is to help her begin to notice her own writing and to begin to want to correct the errors she is capable of fixing.

Independent Activities

Most of this work should be done in a one-on-one setting. There is one independent activity, however, that students do enjoy and that helps them develop their self-editing skills. For this work, prepare a short piece of writing that contains five to eight errors of one type. Then, tell the student the kind of mistakes that are present and challenge him to find them. Three independent activity sheets, "Find My Mistakes," illustrate this work. They are provided on pages 138–140.

Teaching Self-Editing at the Advanced Level

The procedure for teaching self-editing skills at the highest level (items 9–12 in the sequence) is a much more informal method. Focus on one of the elements at a time. For example, you might decide to work on helping a student do a more effective job with transitions in her writing.

Talk with your student about the area. As you sit with her, write a paragraph or two that models this skill. Next, read aloud an area of your student's work where the transitions are good. Then, read aloud a part where some improvement is needed. Talk with your student about the issue, and see if she can hear the problem. If she cannot, do more modeling. If she can, guide her as she improves her work.

This work should be done in a relaxed way. The most important aspect is to help the student begin to notice any confusion or awkwardness in her own writing. It often takes many discussions for a writer to become fully aware of these aspects of her work, because she knows what she meant to say. She knows how the ideas flow.

Even very advanced writers often have difficulty with these skills. Therefore, expect only to begin this process. As long as discussion continues, your student will improve.

Find My Mistakes

In the following story, there are eight missing capitals at the beginning of sentences. See if you can find and correct all of them.

Sarah sighed and looked around. it was true. she was lost. She had walked too far into the forest. It was getting late. it was getting dark.

sarah sat down under a pine tree. she felt like crying, but then she heard a sound. It was the stream that would lead her back to the campsite. sarah got up. she wiped her eyes. she took a deep breath. Sarah started off on her journey back home.

Name _____   Date _____

Find My Mistakes

In the following paragraphs, there are seven mistakes with periods and question marks at the ends of sentences. Some may be missing. Some may be incorrectly used. See if you can find and correct all of them.

Tarantulas are fascinating creatures They are a type of spider. Their body has two main parts which are called the cephalothorax and the abdomen? Tarantulas have eight legs. Did you know that tarantulas molt like a snake does. Adult tarantulas usually molt once or twice a year?

Tarantulas are very large spiders, and they can seem frightening In spite of that, many people keep them as pets. Why do you think some people might enjoy these unusual animals. Would you like to have a tarantula living in your home

Name _____   **Date** _____

Find My Mistakes

In the following paragraphs, you will find eight incomplete sentences. These are sentences that are missing either a subject or a predicate, or both. See if you can find and correct all of them.

Many Chinese men came as immigrants to the United States. In the 1800s. They were very poor. They. Did not have much money. Worse still, they usually had to leave their wives and children in China. Because of the immigration laws.

These men did bring something of great value, however. They brought their stories. These tales helped them. Remember home. They, also. Helped them figure out how to manage in the new country. Fortunately, we can now read these stories. In many books.

Name _____   **Date** _____

WRITING POETRY

Students vary greatly in their responses to poetry. Some see it as humorous word play, while others want to express deep feelings and insight with it. Some express their thoughts literally, while others use abstract images. Some need structure as they begin to approach writing poetry. Others can sit right down and write a poem freely.

Poetry should be an important part of the program for some, since they feel great satisfaction when they can express themselves through this form. For others, poetry is an excellent change of pace for times when some diversity in the programming is needed.

You will soon know in which categories your students belong, since they are generally very vocal about how they feel about poetry. Whatever their approaches are, however, poetry can be a very enjoyable experience for all of them; it just needs to be approached differently for different students. Once they start, many of them demonstrate a real interest in this artistic form.

The activities listed in this section are intended for students who need structure as they begin to work. First, however, we will discuss the students who come to you with the ability to express themselves freely.

For these students, there are two important ways to encourage interest and development:

- Read many good poems to them.
- Give them time to write.

READING POEMS

When you read poems, it is particularly good to select a poem about a certain subject, such as "friendship" or "shadows" or "the moon." Read the poem aloud and discuss some of the images. Then, invite your student to write her own poem on the subject. If she prefers to write on her own topic, that is fine. The reading is only an invitation.

You can find excellent poetry books in your local library. Go and browse and see what is easily available. The following books are particularly good, and are worth trying to obtain through interlibrary loan if they are not in your library.

Even though many of them are either picture books or collections intended for children, they contain many poems that can inspire older students.

1. *City in All Directions*, an anthology of modern poems, edited by Arnold Adoff, drawings by Donald Carrick (Macmillan, 1969). This collection of poems about the city will help students see that poetry is just as important in the city as it is in the country.

2. *Custard and Company: Poems* by Ogden Nash, selected and illustrated by Quentin Blake (Little, Brown, 1980). This very funny collection of poems is made even better by the lively and humorous drawings.

3. *Poetry for Young People*, by Carl Sandburg, edited by Frances Schoonmaker Bolin, illustrated by Steven Arcella (Sterling Publishing Company, 1995). This beautifully illustrated picture book presents favorite and very accessible poems by Carl Sandburg.

4. *The Earth Is Painted Green, a Garden of Poems About Our Planet*, edited by Barbara Brenner, illustrated by S. D. Schindler (A Byron Preiss Book, Scholastic, 1994). This collection of poems will inspire students to notice nature. It even contains a humorous but meaningful poem about pollution.

5. *Old Possum's Book of Practical Cats* by T. S. Eliot, drawings by Edward Gorey (Harcourt Brace Jovanovich, 1939, copyright renewed 1967, illustrations copyright 1982). This classic favorite is sure to interest any of your students who enjoy cats. They'll also laugh.

6. *I Heard a Scream in the Street*, edited by Nancy Larrick (Yearling Book, Dell Publishing Co., Inc., 1970). It can be difficult to find this book, but it is well worth the effort. It is a fine collection of poems written by urban children about their environments.

7. *If You Ever Meet a Whale*, poems selected by Myra Cohn Livingston, illustrated by Leonard Everett Fisher (Holiday House, 1992). This compelling picture book contains a fine selection of poems about whales.

8. *The Random House Book of Poetry for Children, a Treasury of 572 Poems for Today's Child*, selected and introduced by Jack Prelutsky, illustrated by Arnold Lobel, opening poems for each section especially written for this anthology by Jack Prelutsky (Random House, 1983). This anthology is particularly helpful because it has its poems organized in thematic sections. The wide range of selections is excellent.

9. *Something Big Has Been Here*, poems by Jack Prelutsky, drawings by James Stevenson (Greenwillow Books, 1990) and *The New Kid on the Block*, poems by Jack Prelutsky, drawings by James Stevenson (Greenwillow Books, 1984). Both of these book contain very funny poems which your students will enjoy.

10. *Where the Sidewalk Ends,* the poems and drawings of Shel Silverstein (Harper and Row, 1974), and *The Light in the Attic,* poems and drawings by Shel Silverstein (Harper and Row, 1981) and *Falling Up,* poems and drawings by Shel Silverstein (HarperCollins, 1996). These classic collections of humorous poems will delight students of all ages.

ACTIVITIES

The following activities provide structure for students as they begin to write poetry. Often, a particular student will enjoy one structure more than another. He can, therefore, continue using this structure as long as he wishes. Some students who write poetry freely also enjoy experimenting with these activities.

1. **Write a first-letter game poem.** In this kind of poem, a word or phrase is written on the vertical, one letter to a line. The poet then begins each line of the poem with the first letter which is thus provided. For example, if a student named Beth is writing such a poem using her name as the base, she might write:

> Baseball star.
> Expects a lot out of life,
> Talks a lot, but wisely!
> Has fun at school.

Students can use any number of stimulus lines for their poems. Some good word bases are:

- a student's name, as shown above
- the name of a friend or family member
- the name of a famous person
- the name of a pet
- a season of the year
- a holiday
- a feeling, like "loneliness"
- a famous event, like the World Series
- a natural phenomenon, like "hurricane"
- a subject area, like "mathematics"

In a slight variation of the first letter poem, a phrase is being used as the stimulus line. The phrase is written out horizontally as the first line of the poem, and is then repeated vertically, one letter per line, as with the word poems. For example, the phrase "I wish" would look like this:

I wish

w

i

s

h

The repetition of the first line helps students keep their focus on their poem. Some other good phrases to use for first-letter game poems are:

- In one hundred years

- If the world were perfect

- When dinosaurs walked

- Friends are

- Never will I ever

Students can use the dictionary to help them think of great words with which to begin their lines. They can just look up the first letter and see what's there. Also, groups of students sometimes enjoy working on a cooperative poem of this type.

An independent activity sheet, "Never Will I Ever" for a first-letter game poem is provided on page 153.

2. **Write an alphabet poem.** This is a kind of first-letter game poem, where the alphabet is written vertically, one letter per line. Each line of the poem then begins with the letter provided.

The possibilities for the subjects for this kind of poem are unlimited. For example, students can write poems about:

- food

- sports

- countries

- people's names

- jobs.

The following is a wonderful example of this type of poem. It is taken with permission from *The Game of Words* by Willard R. Espy (Grossett & Dunlap, 1972).

AN ANIMAL ALPHABET

Alligator, beetle, porcupine, whale,
Bobolink, panther, dragon-fly, snail,
Crocodile, monkey, buffalo, hare,

Dromedary, leopard, mud-turtle, bear,
Elephant, badger, pelican, ox,
Flying-fish, reindeer, anaconda, fox,
Guinea-pig, dolphin, antelope, goose,
Hummingbird, weasel, pickerel, moose,
Ibex, rhinoceros, owl, kangaroo,
Jackal, opossum, toad, cockatoo,
Kingfisher, peacock, anteater, bat,
Lizard, ichneumon, honey-bee, rat,
Mocking-bird, camel, grasshopper, mouse,
Nightingale, spider, cuttle-fish, grouse,
Ocelot, pheasant, wolverine, auk,
Periwinkle, ermine, katydid, hawk,
Quail, hippopotamus, armadillo, moth,
Rattlesnake, lion, woodpecker, sloth,
Salamander, goldfinch, angleworm, dog,
Tiger, flamingo, scorpion, frog,
Unicorn, ostrich, nautilus, mole,
Viper, gorilla, basilisk, sole,
Whippoorwill, beaver, centipede, fawn,
Xantho, canary, polliwog, swan,
Yellowhammer, eagle, hyena, lark,
Zebra, chameleon, butterfly, shark.

Author unknown

Students love this poem for its humor and its imaginative use of animal names. They also enjoy researching some of the lesser known animals, such as the "ichneumon." Their poems do not have to rhyme, as this one does, but they can add this challenge if they wish to do so.

As with the other types of first-letter game poems, students can use the dictionary to help them think of good words to use. They can also write these poems cooperatively with peers.

An independent activity sheet, "An Alphabet Poem," is provided on pages 154–155.

3. **Write a shape poem.** This idea was discovered in *Really Writing!, Ready-to-Use Writing Process Activities for the Elementary Grades,* by Cherlyn Sunflower (The Center for Applied Research in Education, 1994). Gratitude is expressed to the author, since this type of poem has proven very popular with students with special needs. Most students seem to enjoy this kind of poem, regardless of their writing level.

To write a shape poem, first ask students to think of a specific object that is easy to draw with simple lines, and that makes them think of many words and images. Some good objects are:

- a pizza (See page 147 for an example.)

- any type of sports equipment, such as a basketball

- a shoe

- a book

- a star

- a simple flower

- a fish

- a cat

- a turtle

- a spider

- a snake

- a mud puddle

- a city sidewalk

- a simple building

Ask students to draw their objects on an 8½″ × 11″ piece of paper, so that the drawing fills up much of the page. Then, have each student brainstorm images with you and his peers that are appropriate to his drawing. He then selects favorite images and writes them along the lines of his drawing.

See the "Pizza Poem" example on page 147. An independent activity sheet for a shape poem, "A City Poem," is offered on page 156.

4. **Write a follow-the-pattern poem.** The pattern should be simple and clear. It should help students relax—even students who are initially uncomfortable with writing poetry. The following patterns are good:

- **The months of the year.** Students can choose one month and write a poem about that time of year, or they can name all the months and then state something about each one.

- **The days of the week.** As with months, students can choose one or several days with which to work.

- **Colors.** Students can write about one or several colors. Wonderful examples of this type of poem can be found in *The Palm of My Heart: Poetry by African American Children*, edited by Davida Adedjouma, illustrated by Gregory Christie, introduction by Lucille Clifton (Lee and Low Books, Inc., 1996). This picture book has a selection of poems about what the color *black* means to the poets. It is a joyful book, full of hope and pride.

A Pizza Poem
(a shape poem)

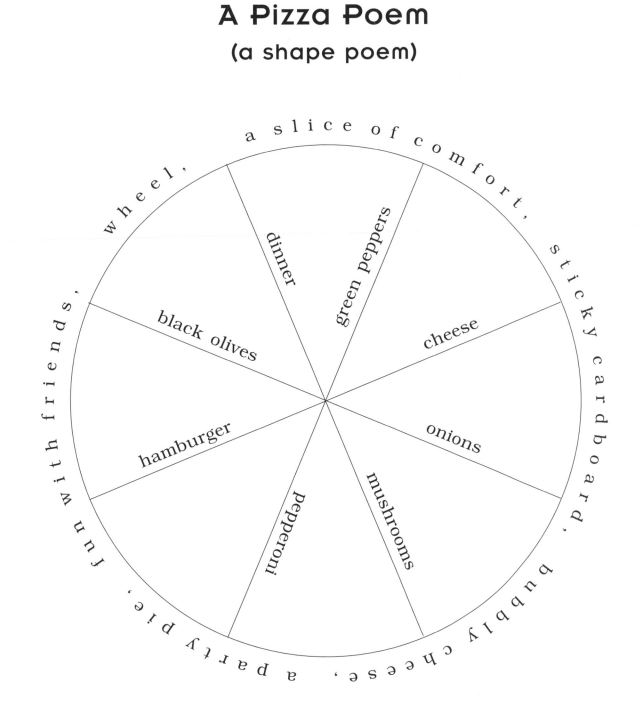

a slice of comfort, sticky cardboard, bubbly cheese, a party pie, fun with friends, wheel,

green peppers
dinner
black olives
cheese
hamburger
onions
pepperoni
mushrooms

- **A pattern of numbers.** Numbers can be used to create many writing patterns. You can ask students to write a poem that has a number at the beginning of each line, such as:

  Two trees watch the nighttime sky,
  Four birds sleep.
  Six . . . and so on.

  You can also create a special format, where you provide the students with a setting in which ten animals or people are doing something. You then ask them to write a poem that tells what happens next. Here is the way such a poem would start:

setting:	Ten cats sat on a barnyard fence.
the action:	The first went this way,
	The second went that.
	The third caught a big fat mouse.
	The fourth raced past him into the house.
	The fifth . . . and so on.

  As always, the rhyming is optional.

- **A pattern of words.** You can create your own simple pattern, such as:

  If I were a _____ ,
  I would _____ .

  An example follows:

  > If I were an airplane,
  > I would soar.
  > If I were an eagle,
  > I would swoop.

  By repeating this phrase with different words and images, students can create meaningful poems of which they feel proud.

  An independent activity sheet that illustrates using one kind of word pattern, "A Pattern Poem," is provided on page 157.

5. **Write an event poem.** This activity was invented by Hedy Christenson, the Director of Eagle Mountain School, Greenfield, Massachusetts. Hedy had gone on a backpacking trip to the High Sierra Mountains and had taken many slides on her trip. She showed selected slides to her students and then asked them to write down words and images that came to mind while they watched each slide. Once the words and images were recorded, students used them to create free verse poetry.

This activity can be varied in many ways. Students can bring in pictures or slides of events that have occurred in their lives. If there is no access to a camera, students can draw pictures of things that they have done, or they can find pictures in magazines, newspapers, and other publications, and these can be used as the stimuli for poems.

Students at all levels of writing skill can work on these poems. Some will create poems full of abstract images. Others will literally record what they see. If students have difficulty with the free verse format, and in fact have difficulty writing any poems once they have recorded their images, another option is to draw pictures of the event that has occurred. Give as much support as is needed at this phase of the work. Students can then record their words and images anywhere on their drawings. See the example of such a poem, "A Backpacking Trip," on page 150.

Students can be very creative with this kind of drawing poem. For example, one student at Eagle Mountain School made a hiking trail of words and images for the backpacking trip. His words traveled in a line all over his paper, just as a hiker would travel on a mountain.

6. **Write a description poem.** You can introduce this kind of poem once students are familiar with nouns and verbs. The poem follows a structured format, in which the first line consists of a noun. In the second line, three present-tense verbs tell what the noun can do. The third line is a short sentence that tells about the noun. The fourth line is another noun that describes the first one in an unusual way. An example of this kind of poem follows:

Song
Reaching, touching, holding
It has no fingers.
Spiderweb

Use the independent activity sheet, "A Tell-It-Like-It-Is Poem," on page 158.

7. **Write a theme poem.** This is a basic and very important type of poem. It relies on and utilizes published poems and, therefore, enriches a student's experience of literature. For this kind of poem, you select and read either one or more poems that deal with a particular topic. These topics are as wide as the human experience. Two examples are:

• The poem "I Should Have Stayed in Bed Today," by Jack Prelutsky from the book *Something Big Has Been Here,* poems by Jack Prelutsky, drawings by James Stevenson (Greenwillow Books, 1990). This humorous poem describes one of those terrible days in which every little thing seems to go

A Backpacking Trip
(an event poem)

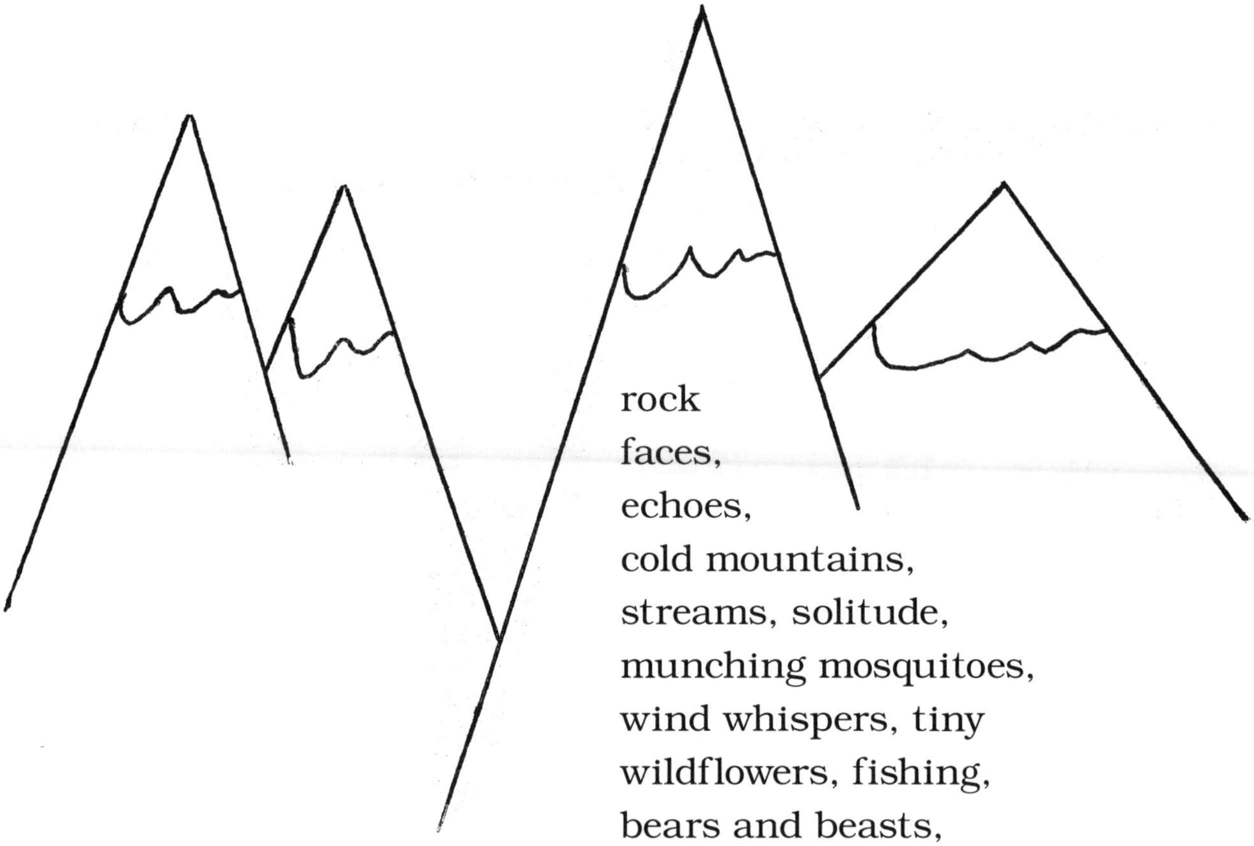

rock
faces,
echoes,
cold mountains,
streams, solitude,
munching mosquitoes,
wind whispers, tiny
wildflowers, fishing,
bears and beasts,
green pine trees

wrong. Students can usually identify with this poem, and enjoy writing about some of the funny things that have happened to them.

- The poem "Arithmetic" by Carl Sandburg, which can be found in the book *Poetry for Young People* by Carl Sandburg, edited by Frances Schoonmaker Bolin, illustrated by Steven Arcella (Sterling Publishing Company, 1995). Students will be surprised to discover the thoughts that Carl Sandburg has had about arithmetic, and they may wish to write on the subject, too.

This technique of selecting good poems, reading them to students and letting them write on the same theme is the same technique that is used with students who come to you with the ability to write poetry freely. As with all techniques, however, this one can be used with differing levels of support. For students who are not yet comfortable with writing poetry, it will help if the poems are easily accessible to them as readers, and if there is a somewhat regular pattern to the language. For instance, in the first example cited above, the difficult happenings are told in the first person. In the second example, Carl Sandburg begins many lines with "Arithmetic is . . ." Students can follow these patterns with their own poems.

There are some wonderful picture books that present several poems about one theme. One such book is *If You Ever Meet a Whale,* poems selected by Myra Cohn Livingston, illustrated by Leonard Everett Fisher (Holiday House, 1992). This book presents a collection of poems about this amazing mammal.

8. **Write rhyming couplets.** Even though rhyming in poetry is never required in *Let's Write!* some students really want to try this challenge. Often, this is difficult for them. The following idea was discovered in *Write! Write! Write!, Ready-to-Use Writing Process Activities for Grades 4–8,* by Carol H. Behrman (The Center for Applied Research in Education, 1995). Gratitude goes to the author, as this technique makes writing rhymes accessible to most students.

Present a series of couplets to your students, each with a missing rhyming word. Some examples follow:

There's a pimple on my chin,
And it does not make me _____ .

The place of our birth
Is the _____ .

Nothing was in sight,
Because it was the dark of _____ .

Sometimes a child
Likes to act _____ .

On a rainy day,
It can be cold and _____ .

The plane flew up there
Into the _____ .

Once the couplets are completed, ask your students if they would like to write their own. If they want to do so, first brainstorm some pairs of rhyming words. Then, either individually or together, make up some poems. Students enjoy illustrating the couplets they create.

Use the independent activity sheet, "Rhyming Pairs," on page 159.

9. **Write a poem full of lies.** This poem is a humorous one in which every line contains a very obvious lie. For example, the poem could begin:

> A cactus is huggable.
> It lives in the frozen North.
> It likes to wave to strangers,
> And to drive a tractor trailer truck.

Some students enjoy illustrating their creations. This is another poem that students enjoy doing as a group activity. An independent activity sheet, "A Poem Full of Lies," is provided on page 160.

Never Will I Ever

Write a "Never will I ever" poem. Begin each line with the letter that is placed at the beginning. Remember, only list things that you will never, ever do. For example, you probably will never:

Expect a rhinoceros to be a ballet dancer, or

Visit and have tea with the Loch Ness monster.

N ever will I ever:

E _____

V _____

E _____

R _____

W _____

I _____

L _____

L _____

I _____

E _____

V _____

E _____

R _____

Name _____ **Date** _____

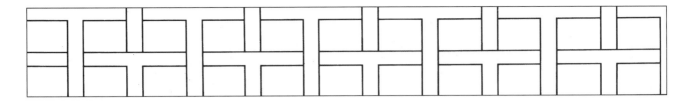

An Alphabet Poem

Write an alphabet poem about the weather by starting each line with the letter that is placed at the beginning. You could start like this:

Always sunny,

Becoming partly cloudy in the afternoon,

Cold,

Damp.

Remember, you can use a dictionary to find good words if you need them.

A __ _____

B _____

C _____

D _____

E _____

F _____

G _____

H _____

I _____

An Alphabet Poem (continued)

J _____

K _____

L _____

M _____

N _____

O _____

P _____

Q _____

R _____

S _____

T _____

U _____

V _____

W _____

X _____

Y _____

Z _____

Name _____ **Date** _____

A City Poem

Use this drawing of a city skyline to write a shape poem about the city. You can use words and images like these:

- people walking
- music on the sidewalk
- tall buildings that talk to the sky

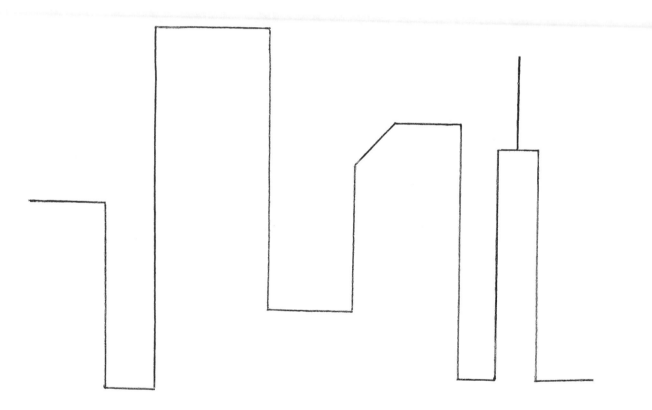

Name _____ **Date** _____

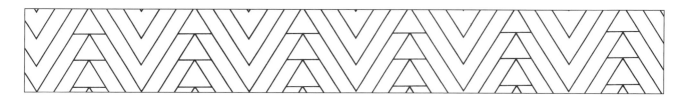

A Pattern Poem

In this three-line poem, the last image of the first line becomes the first image of the next, and so on. For example:

A book is an invitation.
An invitation is an empty box.
An empty box is a cardboard embrace.

You can either finish the poems that are started below or write your own.

A cat is _____

_____

_____

A roller coaster ride is _____

_____

_____

A hot day in the city is _____

_____

_____

Write your own poem below.

_____

_____

_____

_____

_____

Name _____ **Date** _____

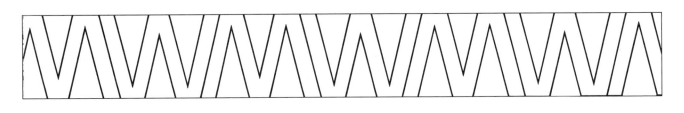

A Tell-It-Like-It-Is Poem

For the first line of this poem, choose a noun. For the second line, write three verbs ending with "ing" that tell what your noun can do. For the third line, write a short sentence. For the fourth line, choose another noun that describes the first in an unusual way. Here is an example:

Basketball
Turning, dribbling, jumping,
It looks like a dance.
Tornado

Write one or more poems here:

_____

_____

_____

_____

_____

_____

_____

_____

_____

_____

_____

Name _____ **Date** _____

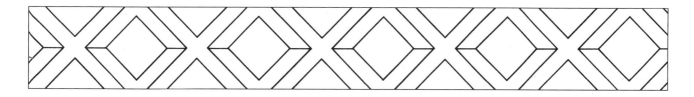

Rhyming Pairs

Finish the following couplets with words that rhyme.

A good boat   Candy is sweet

Can _____ .   To _____ .

I feel lots of gloom,

Because I have to sweep with this _____ .

It's a wonderful thing

To hear a bird _____ .

In the city nights,

There are many _____ .

Now try writing some couplets of your own. Start by listing pairs of rhyming words such as "walking" and "talking," and then see if you can make up some good poems.

_____

_____

_____

_____

_____

_____

_____

_____

Name _____   **Date** _____

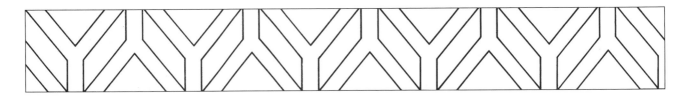

A Poem Full of Lies

Write a poem that is full of lies. See if you can get a really outrageous lie in
every line. Here is one way a lying poem could begin:

> Elephants are tiny,
> They eat delicious stones,
> They like to go to the opera,
> And play bingo with their noses.

Either continue with this one, or start a new lying poem here:

_____

_____

_____

_____

_____

_____

_____

_____

_____

_____

_____

_____

_____

Name _____ **Date** _____

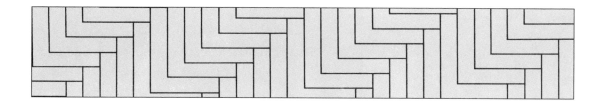

THE LITERATURE
CONNECTION

Published books can greatly assist the development of your students' writing skills. In this section, the focus will be on various types of literature and the specific activities that can be generated from them. Individual books will be cited to illustrate the activities presented, but the main focus is on how to utilize genres of literature. In this way, you will be able to use the books that are readily available to you.

ACTIVITIES

Some individual books cited here are so useful that you may decide to either find them in a library or purchase them. The main goal of this section, however, is to help you use your imagination so that you can develop excellent writing activities with the books that you already have.

1. **Read folk tales and stories.** This type of literature provides excellent stimulation for the writing of lists. These stories are often short, and therefore provide a nice, quick introduction to list writing at the beginning of class. The list idea should be generated from the story.

    For example, an excellent folk tale book is *Thirty-Three Multicultural Tales to Tell* by Pleasant DeSpain, illustrated by Joe Shlichta (a Merrill Court Press Book published by August House Publishers, Inc., 1993). One of the stories, "The Tug of War, a Tale From Africa," tells of how a tortoise uses his brains to outsmart a hippo and an elephant. After hearing this story, students could write a list of jungle animals.

    "Granddaughter's Sled, a Tale From Russia," is the story of how the wisdom of old age comes to be appreciated. For this tale, students could write a list of things that are very old.

    In the story "The Magic Pot, a Tale From China," everything that is placed in the pot is doubled. For this activity, it's fun to bring a "magic pot" to class and pretend that the magic works. Students can enjoy seeing

162   *The Literature Connection*

peanuts or other objects double. They can then write a list of things they would like to put in the magic pot.

2. **Read picture books with predictable patterned text.** These books are wonderful for beginning readers to enjoy, and they are also excellent for beginning writers. In this type of picture book, a pattern of language is repeated over and over.

    First, read such a picture book to your students and enjoy the story with them. Then, help them recognize the language pattern that is repeated throughout. Last, ask them to write their own variations on this pattern. Sometimes it helps to create an activity sheet on which some of the pattern is recorded, and students fill in words that vary the story. You must be aware of copyright laws that protect original text. It is acceptable to use the concept of the pattern that is in a published book, but specific language should not be copied unless the specific language is in the public domain.

    As an example of this activity, the book *The Great Big Enormous Turnip* by Alexei Tolstoy (Scott, Foresman and Company, 1976, 1971) tells the tale of a turnip that is so big that many people and animals are enlisted to help pull it up. First, an old man pulls and pulls, but the turnip will not come out. Then, he asks an old woman to help, and she pulls the man who pulls the turnip, but the turnip will not come out. Next, the old woman asks her granddaughter, and so on. It takes the pull of a little mouse who pulls on a cat who pulls on a dog who pulls on the granddaughter to finally harvest the vegetable.

    For the variation of this pattern, students can decide on the cast of characters they wish to have pull and pull. They may wish to have a rock star start the pulling, and then have a giraffe and a caterpillar get into the act. They can write their stories in a picture-book format and illustrate the action if they wish to do so.

    An independent activity sheet for *The Great Big Enormous Turnip,* "A Turnip Story," is provided on page 169. This activity sheet is appropriate for students working at the word writing level.

3. **Read tall tales.** These exciting stories of obvious exaggeration can invite new writers to invent their own questionable statements and stories. The activity can be varied according to the writing levels of your students.

    For beginning writers who are working on word writing skills, prepare tall tales statements that are missing one word. These statements can follow a pattern like this:

    My brother is so strong, he can lift fifteen _____.

    The independent activity sheet "Don't Lie a Little, Lie a Lot" offers some of these statements (see page 170).

For students working on sentence writing skills, prepare a series of statements that follow this pattern:

My cat is so fast, she _____

_____

Use the independent activity sheet "More Lies" on page 171.

Students who are working on paragraph skills and beyond can try writing tall tales of their own.

Two tall tales that students at all levels will enjoy are the picture books *Pecos Bill, a Tall Tale Told and Illustrated* by Steven Kellogg (William Morrow, 1986) and *Paul Bunyan, a Tall Tale Retold and Illustrated* by Steven Kellogg (William Morrow, 1984). Simon & Schuster also produce a minibook and cassette of *Paul Bunyan* told by Jonathan Winters, adapted by Brian Gleeson, illustrated by Rick Meyerowitz, music by Leo Rottke.

4. **Read picture books that have sophisticated and detailed art.** These books offer opportunities for students to practice their sentence and paragraph writing skills.

   First, read the whole book and enjoy its story. Then, with your students, select an illustration to discuss. They can then write sentences about what they see in the picture. Students who are just beginning to write sentences can follow these repeating formats:

   • I like the _____ in the picture.

                or

   • I see a _____ in the picture.

   Writers who do not need such structure can write sentences freely about the picture.

   Students who are working on paragraph writing skills can discuss what is happening in the picture. They can also discuss the art if they choose to do so; for example, they could begin with the topic sentence:

   • I admire the art in this picture for the following reasons.

   Students often enjoy selecting and writing about several pictures in a favorite book. If chosen carefully for sophisticated art, picture books can even be used in this way for older students.

   A wealth of beautiful picture books is available. One particularly interesting book that has alternating color and black-and-white illustrations is *Clancy's Coat* by Eve Bunting, illustrations by Lorinda Bryan Cauley (Viking Kestrel, 1984). This book tells the story of two Irish neighbors who resolve their differences with the help of an old coat.

5. **Read humorous chapter books and short novels.** These books are great for inspiring "What if I were" paragraphs or stories. First, read such a book during read-aloud time. When finished, discuss the basic humorous situation in which the characters find themselves. Students can then either:

   - write a paragraph or short essay about what they would do if they were in the situation, or

   - make up a story pretending that they are a character who is facing such a challenge.

   An example of such a humorous story is *How to Eat Fried Worms* by Thomas Rockwell, pictures by Emily McCully (Franklin Watts, 1973). Billy, the hero, makes a bet that he can eat one worm a day for fifteen days. The stakes: fifty dollars.

   Billy figures that he's eaten salmon loaf, so how bad can worms be? Besides, fifty dollars is a lot of money. The job turns out to be a bit harder than Billy imagined, and he thinks up some amazing ways to cope with his problem.

   If your students choose to write about what they would do if they were faced with such a dilemma, they can discuss one or more of the following questions:

   - What would they do if someone proposed such a bet to them?

   - What would they do if they had, at a weak moment, made such a bet and then regretted it later?

   - What would they do if a good friend of theirs made such a bet?

   If students choose to write a story inspired by this book, they can pretend they're either Billy or his friend Tom, or the diabolical bettors Alan and Joe. Since in the book there is much attention given to how the worm cuisine is prepared, some students have a lot of fun making up wonderful worm recipes.

6. **Read books written from the point of view of an animal.** Students enjoy these books because they are so often warm and inviting. Two writing activities that spin off well from them are the following:

   - Students can write a letter from one animal to another in the story. The "writer" can either discuss an event that has occurred in the book or make up a new situation or event.

   - Students can write a short story from the point of view of an animal. They can choose a character from the story and write about new events, or they can select a new animal who is introduced to the other characters.

   Two wonderful examples of this type of book are *Rabbit Hill* by Robert Lawson (Viking Press, 1944) and its sequel *The Tough Winter* by Robert

Lawson (Viking Press, 1954). Readers cannot resist Little Georgie, the rabbit, and his worrying mother and gentleman father. Then, there are all the other animals, like Porkey the Woodchuck and Willie Fieldmouse, who tell us how they feel about things through their conversations with each other.

It sometimes helps students begin to write if you first pose some questions for them so that they can begin thinking like their animal. For example, what is the animal's favorite food for supper? Would he be happy or unhappy about a fox moving into the neighborhood? What's her home like? Is it dark and cozy like a burrow, or full of light and fresh air like an open nest? An independent activity sheet that asks some of these questions, "Animal Questions," is offered on page 172.

7. **Read books in which great events occur.** These events can be either humorous or serious. With this type of book, students can write a newspaper article that tells what has happened.

First, read one or two articles about a specific event from your local newspaper. Then, talk with your students about the important elements present in such a piece of writing. Help them discover that articles usually contain the following:

- who or what the story is about

- what happened

- when it happened

For some students, this is adequate preparation. For others who need more challenge, help them discover that people involved in the event are often interviewed and quoted in the story.

Discuss with your student the particular event that she is going to report on from her book. Help her make a brainstorm sheet on which she will record the basic facts she will cover. Then, let her write.

If several students are writing newspaper articles, it's fun to have a TV News Show in which these articles are reported. This should always be a free choice activity, because some students are shy about group presentations.

An example of a humorous book that offers many great events to be covered is *The Hoboken Chicken Emergency* by D. Manus Pinkwater (Aladdin Paperbacks, 1977). When the reservation for the family's Thanksgiving turkey is lost at the meat market, Arthur is sent to find a replacement. Unfortunately, all he can find is a two hundred and sixty-six pound chicken—a *live* two hundred and sixty-six pound chicken! Arthur's mother is understandably reluctant to cook it, and the plot is further complicated by Arthur's growing fondness for the chicken. Students can have great fun writing articles about all the events that occur, especially when the chicken runs away and gets loose in Hoboken.

Based on a true story, *Letters From Rifka* by Karen Hess (Puffin Books, published by the Penguin Group, 1993, Henry Holt, 1992) tells of a Jewish family's escape from persecution in Russia in 1919. Rifka is a twelve-year-old girl who records what happens in a series of letters to her cousin. From the narrow escape at the train station in Berdichev, Russia, to Rifka's detainment on Ellis Island, this story contains many powerful events for students to write about.

8. **Read a middle grade or young adult novel in which serious issues are raised.** These books deal with topics that can have great impact on students' lives. They can cover relationships, moral and ethical, and societal issues such as poverty and racism. For this type of book, students can write their opinions about the topic being raised. Depending on their writing level, they can either write opinion paragraphs or essays.

An example of this type of book is *Z for Zachariah* by Robert C. O'Brien (Atheneum, 1975). This story takes place after a nuclear war in which everyone but the heroine, Ann Burden, is killed—or so she thinks. Protected from the radioactive fallout by a unique geographical situation, Ann has survived while grieving the loss of her family who unwisely left their protected valley. The book opens with Ann being afraid because she worries that another person is entering her valley.

This book is for mature students, because issues of sexual assault and violence are raised, as well as the nuclear holocaust issue. Some older and serious students, however, think a lot about very difficult topics, and it is a good thing to let them know that they can write about their concerns if they wish to do so. It can make writing feel important and empowering to them, and this can definitely assist the development of their writing skills.

9. **Read short excerpts from longer books or read short stories.** Often, these pieces are self-contained snapshots of a particular incident. They are well suited to a writing activity called "What Happens Next?" in which students write their own short stories that begin where the published tale leaves off.

One excellent book containing many good excerpts is *The Random House Book of Humor for Children*, selected by Pamela Pollack, illustrated by Paul O. Zelinsky (Random House, 1988). This book contains parts of books as diverse as *Life Among the Savages* by Shirley Jackson and *Tom Sawyer* by Mark Twain.

An excellent short story, especially for older students is "Thank You, M'am" by Langston Hughes, which can be found in the book *Something in Common and Other Stories* by Langston Hughes (American Century Series, Hill and Wang, a division of Farrar, Straus and Giroux, 1963). This tale relates what happens to a boy who tries to steal a woman's purse. He doesn't succeed, and the reader knows that the boy's life is changed by the kindness and common sense of his intended victim, Mrs. Luella Bates Washington Jones.

But where does the boy go next? What does he do? What happens to Mrs. Jones? Doing a "What Happens Next?" story can make the original text seem more real, as well as provide a meaningful writing experience for your students.

10. **Read a special, humorous book that inspires a unique writing activity.** It's best to always be aware of possible writing activities when you are reading a humorous story, because for some students, the element of silliness can take away their fear of writing. Relax, enjoy the book, and you may think of a wonderful way to use it to encourage your students' writing.

Here are some examples of such books and the unique activities that they inspire:

- *Alexander and the Terrible, Horrible, No Good, Very Bad Day* by Judith Viorst, illustrated by Ray Cruz (Aladdin Books, 1972). This funny picture book chronicles a truly horrible day in the life of Alexander. Everything goes wrong, and students enjoy hearing about his troubles. They can then invent their own stories about a disastrous day.

  It tends to work best if students first make a list of some unfortunate incidents. They can then either write in the first person or create a character to experience the trouble.

  Even though this activity is based on a picture book, older students can also enjoy it. You can reassure them that the picture book just provides the inspiration for their work.

- *That's Good! That's Bad!* by Margery Cuyler, pictures by David Catrow (Henry Holt, 1991). This picture book is based on a folklore tradition called *Good or Bad*. The story begins with a little boy receiving a balloon, which is good, but then all sorts of things that are not necessarily good occur.

  In this folklore tradition, the first statement sets the stage—for example:

  > "Kim was taking a nap."

  The writer then states that this is good. "But no," the writer answers, "This is bad because . . ." and so on.

  An example follows:

  > "Johari went on a camping trip."
  > "That's good."
  > "No, that's bad. There were bears in the woods."
  > "That's bad."
  > "No, that's good. The bears were friendly."
  > "That's good."

"No, that's bad. The bears were also hungry."

"That's bad."

"No, that's good. Johari . . ." and so on.

This activity can be done with two people, one taking the "good" and one the "bad" side. It can also be done with teams of people, or with just one writer creating a series of events. Use the independent activity sheet "Good or Bad?" on page 173.

- The poem "Sarah Cynthia Sylvia Stout Would Not Take the Garbage Out" by Shel Silverstein from the book *Where the Sidewalk Ends,* the poems and drawings of Shel Silverstein (HarperCollins, 1974). This poem lists in great detail the odious food products that accumulate when Sarah Cynthia Sylvia Stout refuses to take out the trash. And what finally happens? Well, students have to read the whole poem to find out.

  Students who enjoy this type of humor like to make up lists of the various items of garbage that they can imagine accumulating. They then make up their own poems.

  This activity works very well as a group project, because then lots of ideas can be gathered for the poem. If students want their lines to rhyme, some teacher assistance is usually required.

- *Freckle Juice* by Judy Blume, illustrated by Sonia O. Lisker (A Yearling Book, Bantam Doubleday Dell Books for Young Readers, 1971). Andrew wants freckles like his friend Nicky who has tons of them, because then Andrew's mother will never be able to tell if he has a dirty neck. So Andrew pays Sharon the fifty cents she demands for her secret freckle formula. Does it work? Perhaps. Perhaps not.

  Students can enjoy making up their own freckle juice formula. This is a good activity for students working at all levels—even students working on word writing skills.

- *Chocolate Fever* by Robert Kimmel Smith, illustrated by Gioia Fiammenghi (A Yearling Book, Bantam Doubleday Dell Books for Young Readers, 1972). Henry loves chocolate, and he eats it every day—in his cereal, his sandwiches, and his mashed potatoes. Henry eats so much chocolate, in fact, that one day he develops beautiful brown spots all over his body. How does Henry get rid of them? Does Henry ever get rid of them? This book raises many questions.

  Students can enjoy writing a daily menu that includes some interesting foods with chocolate. Pizza with chocolate chips, anyone? This activity is good for students working at all levels of their writing development— even word writing skills.

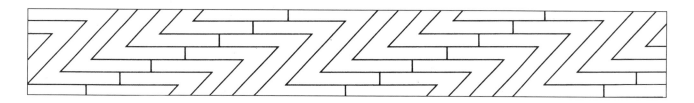

A Turnip Story

Now that you have read <u>The Great Big Enormous Turnip</u>, you can write your own story using this book as inspiration. Fill in the blanks and then, if you wish, illustrate your story on a separate sheet of paper.

Once, a long time ago, a _____ tried to harvest a huge turnip. It was the biggest turnip the _____ had ever grown. The _____ pulled, but the turnip stayed in the ground. So the _____ asked some friends to help.

A _____ pulled the _____, but the turnip would not come out. Then, a _____ pulled the _____ who pulled the _____, but the turnip would still not come out.

A _____ pulled the _____ who pulled the _____ who pulled the _____, but the turnip was still in the ground. Finally, a _____ pulled the _____ who pulled the _____ who pulled the _____ who pulled the _____, and the turnip came out. They all enjoyed turnip stew for supper.

© 1997 by Cynthia M. Stowe

Name _____   **Date** _____

Don't Lie a Little, Lie a Lot

Finish these statements so that they are definitely not true.

1. The elephant is so big, it is bigger than a _____.

2. The car is so old, it is older than the _____.

3. Charlie is so fast, he can run faster than a _____.

4. The tree is so tall, it is taller than the _____.

5. The mouse is so tiny, he is smaller than a _____.

6. The lake is so deep, it is deeper than the _____.

7. These mashed potatoes are so cold, they are colder than the _____.

8. Mi-Cha is so strong, she can hop up _____ flights of stairs on one foot.

Name _____   **Date** _____

More Lies

Finish these statements so that they are definitely not true.

1. The little boy was so smart, he _____
_____

2. Vera jumped so high, she _____
_____

3. Devin was so hungry, he _____
_____

4. The rhinoceros was so clumsy, he _____
_____

5. The monster was so scary, it _____
_____

6. Maria was so tired, she _____
_____

7. The plane flew so fast, it _____
_____

8. The moon was so bright, it _____
_____

Name _____   **Date** _____

Animal Questions

Before you write from the point of view of an animal, ask yourself the following questions. They will help you get to know your animal better, and this will make writing much easier.

1. How big does a person look to your animal?

2. How would your animal safely cross the road?

3. Where would your animal go on vacation?

4. What would your animal like for a present?

5. How does your animal know what time it is?

6. How would your animal travel across the ocean?

7. If your animal were going to go to the movies, how would she or he get in?

8. What kind of wall posters would your animal choose for his or her own room?

9. What would your animal do if she or he were caught in an elevator?

10. If your animal had to choose a career, would he or she be a plumber, an artist, or a police officer?

Name _____   Date _____

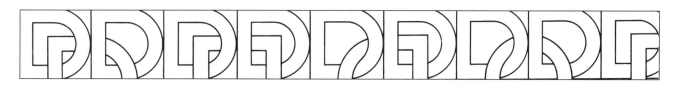

Good or Bad?

<u>GOOD OR BAD?</u> is based on an American folklore tradition. To play this game, first write a sentence that sets the story stage. For example,

"Mario went fishing in the ocean."

Then, you alternate between good and bad statements; for example,

"That's good."
"No, that's bad. A storm started."
"Oh, that's bad."
"No, that's good. Mario had a sturdy boat."
"That's good."
"No, that's bad. The boat . . ." and so on.

You can continue with this <u>GOOD OR BAD?</u> story or start one of your own.

_____

_____

_____

_____

_____

_____

_____

_____

_____

_____

_____

_____

Name _____ **Date** _____

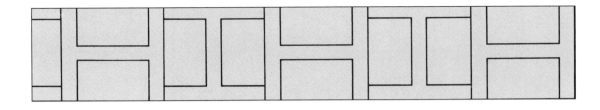

HOLIDAYS

With the multitude of cultures present in the United States, there is a wealth of holiday celebrations. Sometimes, these holidays can appear to be distractions, times when students are excited and very active and not particularly focused on academics. They may feel like times to "get through," because not much academic work will be accomplished.

If approached correctly, however, holidays can offer rich stimulation for writing. If students are interested and motivated by a holiday, they can express some of this positive energy with writing.

Some of the important holidays in the United States, which are widely recognized in this culture, are:

- New Year's Day (Jan. 1)
- Martin Luther King Jr.'s Birthday (third Monday in Jan.)
- Lincoln's Birthday (Feb. 12)
- St. Valentine's Day (Feb. 14)
- Washington's Birthday (third Monday in Feb.)
- St. Patrick's Day (March 17)
- Easter Sunday (between March 22 and April 25)
- Memorial Day (May 30 or last Monday in May)
- Independence Day (July 4)
- Labor Day (first Monday in Sept.)
- Columbus Day (Oct. 12 or second Monday in Oct.)
- Halloween (Oct. 31)
- Veteran's Day (Nov. 11)
- Pamadan (the date varies from Nov. through Jan.)
- Thanksgiving Day (fourth Thursday in Nov.)
- Hanukkah (begins on the 25th of Kislev, the ninth month of the Jewish year, and continues for eight days)
- Christmas (Dec. 25)
- Kwanzaa (begins on Dec. 26 and continues for seven days)

Because of our great diversity, however, there are many other holidays that are less well known. Some examples of these are:

- Gung Hay Fat Choy (Chinese, New Year's Day)
- Robert E. Lee's Birthday (Jan. 19 or third Monday in Jan.)
- New Zealand Day (Feb. 6)
- Greece Independence Day (March 25)
- Pan American Day (April 14)
- Victoria Day (Canadian, May 24)
- Egyptian National Day (July 23)
- Whai Oh! Jamaica Independence Day (first Monday in August)
- The Green Corn Ceremony (many Native American cultures, before the main crop of corn is ready to be harvested)
- Boxing Day (Great Britain, the first working day after Christmas)

Many of these holidays are discussed in the book *Multicultural Discovery Activities for the Elementary Grades* by Elizabeth Crosby Stull (The Center for Applied Research in Education, 1995). This book is an excellent reference for multicultural holidays for the elementary age student. Another valuable reference book is *Celebrations Around the World, a Multicultural Handbook* by Carole S. Angell (Fulcrum Resources, Fulcrum Publishing, 1996).

TALKING ABOUT HOLIDAYS

Teachers who wish to be respectful of all their students' varied cultures and their celebrations sometimes worry that they may fail to pay enough attention to a particular holiday. Because of unfamiliarity with certain cultural backgrounds, they fear that they may place too much emphasis on one holiday to the exclusion of another. The only way to be fair and respectful to all the cultures present in a given classroom is to talk with your students about the issue. Ask them to tell you about the celebrations in their families and communities. Your students have the information you need. Most will feel honored and respected to be asked. If any students show reluctance to discuss these important times, respect their silence, as their reticence may be based on important cultural factors.

Certain holidays that are cherished by some cultures are considered hurtful to others. It's important to be aware of the various feelings that holidays can engender, and to be respectful of all of these feelings.

HOLIDAY ACTIVITIES

Each of the following activities can be used with many different holidays. They are offered in this way so that you can use them for any important holiday in your classroom. This gives a wider range of options than if specific activities were presented for individual celebrations. Some holidays are mentioned with presented activities, but these are included as examples.

1. **Write lists about things associated with a holiday.** List topics can cover a wide range:

   - special foods eaten

   - songs that are sung

   - costumes or special clothing that is worn

   - gifts that can be given

   - decorations that are made

   - beliefs that are discussed

   - activities engaged in

   - values that are honored.

   A particular holiday can inspire a unique list. For example, for Halloween, students can write a list of ingredients that can go into a witch's brew. An independent activity sheet, "What I Found in my Bag after Halloween" is offered on page 180.

2. **Write a shape poem.** This idea is discussed on pages 145–146 in the "Poetry" chapter of this book. For this poem, students either draw a simple picture of an object that is associated with a holiday, or you can provide one for them. Use the picture for "A Candle Poem" on page 181. The candle can be an important image for many holidays, such as Hanukkah and Kwanzaa.

   Once the shape is provided, help students brainstorm some words associated with the holiday. For example, if they are writing a candle shape poem for Kwanzaa, they may think of, "light," "unity," "hope," "creativity," and "seven candles for seven days." Students then select their favorite words and write them along the lines of their candle.

3. **Write a first-letter game poem.** This idea is also discussed on pages 143–144 in the "Poetry" chapter. For this poem, write the holiday's name vertically on the paper, one letter for each line. Students then begin each line of their poem with the first letter present. The following is an example of such a poem for Memorial Day:

   Mourn
   Everyone, please.
   Men and women who died
   On land far and near.
   Remember
   If you can

And
Learn from their deaths.

Day.
At last a day
You can remember and mourn.

This is often a good group activity, since many people can then offer suggestions for good first words. Also, the dictionary can provide help with this part of the work. Students simply look up a letter and find out what words are there.

An independent activity sheet, "A Thanksgiving Poem," is provided on page 182. As a special note concerning this holiday, some people have negative feelings about it because of the way the Native American population was treated by the European settlers. These negative feelings, as well as the positive ones, can be expressed through the poem.

4. **Do an interview on a person's perspective on a holiday.** These interviews fall into two major categories:

   - an interview of an elderly person who can report on how a holiday was celebrated in the past

   - an interview of a person from another culture who can report on how the holiday is celebrated in her world

   Two independent activity sheets, "A Holiday from the Past" and "A Holiday from Another Culture," offer questions for these two interviews (see pages 183 and 184). These are appropriate for students working at all levels, from the word writing level up.

5. **Write a letter from an important person associated with a holiday.** If the holiday celebrates an individual, students assume the persona of that person—Martin Luther King, for example—and write the letter. "He" can write to a particular individual or to a group of people. "He" can cover a wide variety of topics, such as things that happened in "his" life, or "his" opinion about what is happening in our present world.

   Humorous examples of such letters can be found in the book, *J. R. R. Tolkien, the Father Christmas Letters,* edited by Baillie Tolkien (Houghton Mifflin, 1979). This book offers a collection of letters that J. R. R. Tolkien wrote to his children from 1925 through 1938. In them, the author pretended to be Father Christmas (or Santa Claus), and "he" told his children many tales of "his" adventures at the North Pole. These letters were accompanied by illustrations, and placed in specially decorated envelopes with North Pole stamps.

6. **Make a holiday statement quilt.** If you have the sewing skill, the time, and the necessary materials—fabric, fabric paint, and a sewing machine—this

quilt can become a beautiful wall hanging to decorate your classroom for future years. If you wish to, however, you can simply make this quilt out of squares of paper.

This is a group activity in which each participating student is given one square of paper or fabric. Any square from eight to ten inches is a good size. Students then write either phrases or sentences about the holiday on their squares and decorate them. These squares are then bordered by one-and-a-half- to two-inch strips of fabric or paper, and assembled into a quilt.

7. **Write an opinion paragraph or essay.** Some students are serious thinkers who wish to explore and express their thoughts and feelings about a holiday. For this activity, you can propose a series of questions that will generate deep thought. Students can choose one, or can propose a question of their own. Some good questions are:

   • What does (the holiday) mean to you?

   • What could (the holiday) mean to someone who does not value what it represents?

   • What would you do if you were forced to work at your job on (the holiday)?

   • Should anyone be forced to work on (the holiday)?

   • What could you do to help other people understand (the holiday)?

   • What is so special about (the holiday) that makes it be so widely recognized?

   • Does anyone have the right to criticize (the holiday)?

   • Is there a universal holiday that everyone can celebrate?

8. **Write an "I knew him/her when" story.** This activity is good for a holiday that celebrates the life of a famous person. Students first do some research, reading available books and encyclopedias. As much as possible, they collect information about the person's early life. Students then assume the persona of someone who knew the celebrity during the early part of his or her life, and they write an account of their mutual experiences.

   This can be done in either a serious or a humorous way. For the latter, it's fun to pretend that the writer is an animal.

9. **Write an "If They Met" story.** This is another good activity for a holiday in which a person's accomplishments are recognized. For this work, students imagine what it would be like if the honored person met another famous individual. For example, what if George Washington met Abraham Lincoln? What kinds of questions would they ask each other? Would George be surprised that there were so many new states in the United States in the 1860s? Would he know about slavery? These questions offer good opportunities for research.

This activity can be done simply or with much complexity. Students who are capable of writing dialogue can document a conversation between the two people. Students working at the word writing level can have their characters answer specific questions. An independent activity sheet, "If They Met," which illustrates this activity at the word writing level, is provided on page 185.

10. **Write a recipe for a special dish, or a menu for a holiday meal.** In many cultures, food is associated with celebration. Ask your students if they wish to share information about what their families eat during a holiday. This can range from a recipe for a favorite cookie such as a macaroon, to a menu for a whole dinner such as a traditional Polish Christmas Eve supper. Students can write out these recipes and menus, and then you can copy and distribute them.

    As with all activities that involve information about families, you must carefully watch your students' comfort levels. If any student appears anxious or withdrawn, a different activity should be quickly suggested.

11. **Make an art essay with text.** For this activity, students can gather either photographs, their own drawings, or pictures from magazines, newspapers, and other published texts. They can place these pictures into a notebook or a handmade bound book, and then write text to accompany them. The text can tell what is happening in the picture, or can give an opinion about the action. If students are working at the word writing level, they can label portions of the artwork.

12. **Create a special holiday.** Some students may not feel connected to a holiday that is being recognized by the majority culture. These students may wish to create their own special day. This holiday can honor a person, like Harriet Tubman (the amazing woman who escaped from slavery and who then returned to the South to lead many others to freedom), or a group of people, such as people who are nurses. It can even honor a special animal, such as a cat, or a group of animals, such as birds.

    As they create their holiday, students can consider the following:

- What day is the holiday celebrated on?
- Are there rituals for the holiday, such as the lighting of candles?
- Are gifts given, and if so, what kinds of gifts are exchanged?
- Are special songs sung?
- Are special stories told?
- Is unique food prepared at the time?

    Students can write about their holiday and draw pictures about it. They can then, if they wish, present their holiday to their peers.

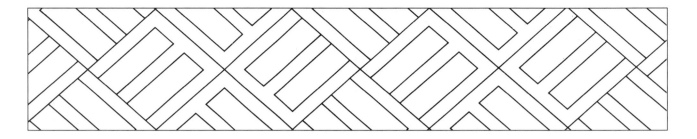

What I Found in My Bag
After Halloween

Have you ever gone Trick-or-Treating and not really noticed the treats you were collecting? Have you been surprised later with what you've found? Make a list of some special things you could be amazed to discover in your Trick-or-Treat bag. You could start your list with "the tooth of a dinosaur."

Name _____   **Date** _____

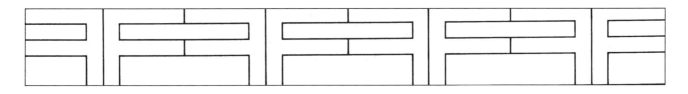

A Candle Poem

Use this drawing of a candle to write a shape poem about your holiday. You can use special words to outline the drawing.

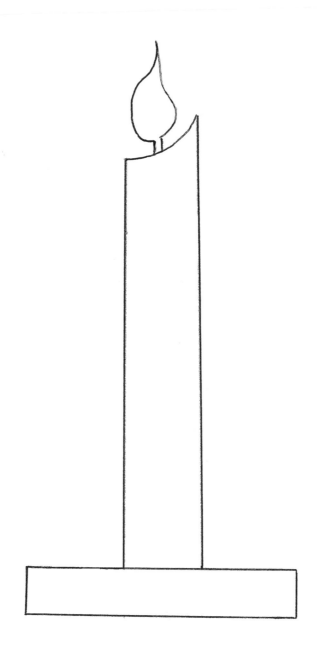

Name _____   **Date** _____

A Thanksgiving Poem

Take the letters of the holiday "Thanksgiving" and begin each line of a poem with that letter. You could start your poem with:

- Thinking of what I have to be grateful for,

- Happy for my friends.

T _____

H _____

A _____

N _____

K _____

S _____

G _____

I _____

V _____

I _____

N _____

G _____

Name _____ **Date** _____

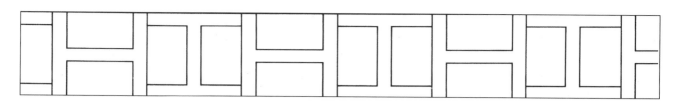

A Holiday from the Past

Use these questions to help you interview an elderly person about a holiday that person remembers from when she or he was young.

1. Did you give or receive gifts? If so, what were some of them?

2. Was the holiday celebrated by everyone where you lived?

3. Were special foods made? If so, what were they?

4. Did people feel differently about the holiday than we do now? If so, how did they feel?

5. What was your favorite thing about the holiday?

6. Was there anything that was difficult about the holiday?

7. How much time did people spend preparing for the holiday?

8. What was done to help people understand the meaning of the holiday?

9. Were any special clothes worn or decorations made? If so, what were they?

10. Can you think of any differences in the way the holiday is celebrated now from when it was celebrated then?

Name _____   **Date** _____

A Holiday from Another Culture

Use these questions to help you interview a person from another culture about a holiday.

1. Do all families in your community celebrate the holiday?

2. If all families celebrate the holiday, do they do so in the same way?

3. Are there special foods eaten at holiday time? If so, what are they?

4. What do people wear for the holiday?

5. Do people exchange gifts? If so, what kinds of gifts are given and received?

6. Are specific rituals performed at holiday time?

7. How do people communicate to young children and to people outside the community what the holiday means?

8. Would you include someone from a different culture in your holiday? If so, how would you do this?

9. Is there something you don't like about the holiday? If so, what is it?

10. Is there something you really like about the holiday? If so, what is it?

Name _____   **Date** _____

If They Met

Imagine that the person who is being honored by a holiday meets another famous person. Then, think about what the answers would be if they asked each other the following questions.

1. Where did you grow up? _____

2. What kind of family did you grow up in? _____

_____

3. What did you do to make a living? _____

_____

4. What was the hardest thing you ever had to do in your life? _____

_____

5. Did you ever think you would be famous? _____

_____

6. What are you most proud of? _____

_____

7. What do you think was your biggest mistake? _____

_____

8. How do you feel about the problems in the modern world? _____

_____

9. What surprises you most about modern life? _____

_____

10. What do you think is the best thing about people? _____

_____

Name _____ **Date** _____

WRITING LETTERS

The ability to write a clear, well-organized letter is an important skill that will help students in both their academic and their regular lives. Students won't necessarily have to write essays and reports once they leave an educational setting. They will, however, always benefit from being able to write a good letter. *Let's Write!* provides instruction for the two main kinds of letters: friendly letters and business letters.

WRITING FRIENDLY LETTERS

Begin by talking with your students about their experiences with friendly letters. Do they write to members of their families—their grandparents, for example? Do they see their parents or other members of their community writing friendly letters?

Once you have gained information on how relevant letter writing has been to your students, talk with them about what the form is meant to convey. Friendly letters can:

- express concern and caring for someone
- ask how the person is doing
- give personal information about activities
- give personal information about feelings

Discuss these purposes informally. If you are comfortable, bring in a friendly letter you have received and share it with your students.

The next step is to discuss the structural parts of the friendly letter. Write a very short letter on the chalkboard or on a large piece of paper, and then show students the following parts:

- the greeting
- the body of the letter
- the closing

This demonstration can be done in a relaxed manner, just to introduce the structure. Students will master it once they write their own letters.

186

The first letter students actually write can be a group letter. Select a person at school with whom everyone feels comfortable. Brainstorm with your students several things they would like to tell this person, and write these ideas down either on the chalkboard or on a large piece of paper.

The issue of where to place the sections of the letter on their own papers can be a problem for some students who have spatial difficulties. To help with this, place small pencil checks where students should start the greeting and the body of the letter on their papers. When they are ready, make a third check that correctly places the closing. Talk about some options for the closing such as "With best regards," and "Yours truly." Once the letter is written, erase the pencil marks. Provide this support for as long as it is needed.

One technique that helps students understand what makes a letter interesting is called "Bad Letter and Better Letter." First, show students an example of a letter that conveys little information and feeling. Then, show them a letter with more content. Discuss with your students which letter they would prefer to receive. What makes the "bad" letter boring? What makes the "better" letter more interesting? One "bad" letter and one "better" letter, illustrating this technique, are provided on page 188.

The degree of modeling and group work that must be done before students start writing friendly letters independently is dependent on both their skill levels and their prior experiences with this form. When they are ready, they can begin to write letters on their own.

WRITING BUSINESS LETTERS

The introduction to this type of letter must be fairly simple. The main purposes of business letters are:

- to request information
- to ask for a product
- to give information
- to convey an opinion

Tell your students that business letters are more formal than friendly letters, and that they also vary in form. They are, however, basically letters, and students should not be intimidated by them. They are, in some ways, easier to write than friendly letters since the purpose for the letter can be clearly and easily stated right at the beginning.

Explain to your students that there are six sections to a business letter:

- the date
- the sender's address

Bad Letter and Better Letter

Would you enjoy receiving this letter?

Dear Pedro,

    How are you? I am fine. My family is fine. My dog is fine. The weather is good here.

    How is your father? How is your dog? How is your weather?

                  Good-bye,

                  Tom

Or would you rather receive this letter?

Dear Henrietta,

    It's been snowing here all day. I have really enjoyed being at home and looking out at our first winter storm.

    Yesterday, Ben and I took a long hike up Mt. Toby. We decided to follow a trail we had never been on, and we got lost. It was getting dark and we were getting scared. But then we stumbled upon the main trail. What a relief!

    Are you doing well in school? I like my job at the Dairy Mart a lot. Write back soon.

                  Fondly,

                  Sonia

- the address of the business
- the greeting
- the body of the letter
- the closing

Model writing a business letter for your students. If you feel comfortable, share with them copies of one or two such letters you have sent in the past.

Decide on a business letter you would like to write as a group. This can be to an organization that advocates for endangered species or to any number of other organizations. If students wish to do so, they can invent a company and a product.

With your students, write a group letter. For students with spatial problems who may have difficulty correctly placing the sections of the letter, put a small pencil checkmark where they should write the date, their address, and the company's address. Some students will need help with putting each part of the address on a separate line. In other words, some students write the company's name on the first line and then continue the street address on the same line. The important thing is to watch your students during this part of the process and to provide as much support as they need.

Once students have successfully placed the first three sections, put small pencil checkmarks where the greeting and the body of the letter should start. When students are ready, provide the same help for the closing. Once the letter is written, erase the pencil marks.

As you are writing your group letter, talk about how the greeting and the closing need to be more formal than in a friendly letter. "Sincerely," makes an excellent closing.

Once the group letter is composed, assess whether your students are ready to practice writing business letters on their own. As with friendly letters, provide as much support as is needed until students are ready to work independently with this form.

A quick note must be added about helping students with spatial problems address envelopes. Ask your students to count how many lines are needed for the address. With a ruler and a pencil, draw the necessary lines on the envelope in the proper place. Do the same for the return address. As soon as possible, ask your students to draw these lines for themselves. These lines help students feel proud of their addresses, because they enable them to write neatly. With repeated use, they also teach students the proper placement of the addresses.

Work with business letters should be done in a relaxed manner. This is an introduction to business letters, and the main thing for students to learn is that there is no mystery to them. There is a structure that must be followed, and the purpose of the letter must be simply stated. Once students understand these two concepts, they will become more comfortable and competent with practice.

The issue of the cost of stamps must also be addressed. This can be a difficult problem; you want your students to be able to mail their letters, but some of them will not have the money to buy stamps.

It often helps to discuss this issue with your school administrator. If you explain the purpose of the unit, he or she may be able to find some way to provide financial support for it. Sometimes parent organizations can offer help, or appropriate school funds can be used.

ACTIVITIES

Some students will happily write many friendly and business letters in class. Others, however, need the excitement of variations on these two basic forms. The following activities are favorites that can stimulate your students to do a great deal of letter writing.

1. **Write a picture postcard.** Students especially enjoy making their own. The U.S. Postal Service requires that a postcard be no smaller than 3½″ × 5″, and no larger than 4¼″ × 6″. Lined index cards, 4″ × 6″, make excellent postcards because they are within the size guidelines, and their paper weight is good. The lined side can be used to help students with spatial issues write neatly and with good spacing.

   Students enjoy decorating the picture side of the postcard with their own drawings, or with cutouts from magazines or newspapers. They can create collages if they wish. The messages on their postcards can discuss their art, or they can simply send friendly greetings.

2. **Send for free items.** Many companies and organizations provide free materials when they are requested to do so. These gifts can range from astronomy booklets to samples of catnip to pictures and other promotional material from sports teams.

   Some students are highly motivated to send for these products, and they gain excellent practice in doing so. One book that lists good organizations to write to is *Free Stuff for Kids, Hundreds of Free and Up-to-a-Dollar Things Kids Can Send for by Mail!* (Meadowbrook Press, Distributed by Simon and Schuster, 1997). This book has been updated every year since 1976. A second book that lists good places for students to write to is *The Official Freebies for Kids, Something for Nothing or Next to Nothing!* by the editors of *Freebies* magazine, illustrations by Anna Pomasca (Lowell House, Juvenile, Contemporary Books, 1995). A 1997 version is scheduled to be released.

As you can see from the subtitles, some of the products in both these books do cost money. There are are also, however, many good free products listed.

3. **Write thank-you notes.** Many things happen in a school year that provide opportunities for these letters. Has someone been a tour guide on a field trip, or have you had a special speaker at school? Has a person donated books or materials to your classroom? Help students brainstorm what they appreciate about whatever gift was made, and let them write thank-you notes.

4. **Write a letter to a teacher.** Ask students to write a letter to you. Ask them to include information on some of the following:

   • What have they enjoyed learning?

   • Has a certain type of work been difficult for them?

   • Would they like some extra help on a particular task?

   • Is there a special subject or topic that they would like to study in your class?

   • Is there something about themselves that they would like to share in their letters?

   If it is possible, it is very reinforcing for you to write back to students. Once they feel comfortable with this form, students can also write letters to other teachers at school.

5. **Write a fan letter to a celebrity.** Help students to brainstorm what they want to say to their selected famous person. They can choose from the following:

   • What do they admire in general about the celebrity?

   • Is there a specific incident or ability that they wish to acknowledge?

   • Do they want to tell the celebrity something about themselves?

   Once students have made notes of the topics they wish to cover, they can begin their letters. Write to the celebrity in care of the organization with which he or she is associated.

6. **Write a letter to an elected official expressing an opinion about a current issue.** These issues can be local, state, or national.

   Ask students to tell you their opinions, and then help them brainstorm reasons for feeling the way they do. Once these reasons are jotted down, they can include them in their opinion letters.

   (*Note:* The activities listed above present letters that can actually be sent. The next six are creative writing activities that are meant to be enjoyable practice experiences.)

7. **Write a letter to the Patent Office, proposing an "interesting" invention.** In this activity, students create an invention. This can be a television that talks. ("Say, don't you think you've watched me long enough? You should get started on your homework.") It can be a basketball that always goes through the hoop when a player wears a special remote-control ring to guide it. The possibilities are endless!

    In their letters, students describe their inventions and the functions they perform. They can also draw pictures and diagrams of the inventions. An independent activity sheet, "Something New," which illustrates this kind of letter, is provided on page 194.

8. **Write a silly letter of complaint.** Ask students to think of a product they have either used in the past week or thought a lot about. Then ask them to imagine how it would feel if everything went wrong with that product. Help them brainstorm and record some of these disasters.

    Have they used a pencil, for example, whose lead broke every time they tried to write? Maybe, when they finally sharpened it for the fifteenth time and the lead seemed okay, the pencil wrote in Spanish when they tried to write in English. That was fine, but the English teacher was upset. And then, when they tried to erase their work, the pencil's eraser shredded the paper.

    Students would have many justifiable complaints to make to a company that produced such a product. Use the independent activity sheet, "It's Horrible!" on page 195.

9. **Write a letter about what you didn't do this past weekend.** Teachers are always telling students to include information about what they have done in their letters to friends. "Did you go to the movies? Great. Well, then, tell Juan about that."

    In this new type of letter, students invent activities they have *not* done, and they are not bound by the laws of reality in their creations. For example, they probably haven't flown above the Andes Mountains in a hot air balloon, or gone to Africa and ridden on a rhinoceros, or seen a UFO when they were walking through the park.

    The independent activity sheet, "Believe It!" illustrates this type of letter and is found on page 196.

10. **Write an "It's Very Strange Here" letter.** Students imagine that they are either visiting another planet, or that they are in an imaginary place on Earth. They write letters back to friends telling them what the place is like.

    Has a student, for example, fallen asleep one afternoon and woken up in a deep forest, where the trees feel soft, like foam rubber, and the clouds are bright yellow. Is there, perhaps, a tiny animal nearby that looks like a baby rabbit, but has antlers and huge teeth?

This activity is good for students working at all levels of writing, because it can be concrete. A student who is working on word writing skills can write a letter greeting, and then, with help, can write the short sentence, "This is what (the name of his planet or place) looks like." He can then draw a picture and label the different parts of his drawing.

An independent activity sheet, "It's Very Strange Here," is provided on page 197.

11. **Write a "These Earth People Are Too Much" letter.** Students pretend that they are visiting aliens, writing back to their friends on planet Ixmus. In their letters, they describe Earth, but particularly they describe the truly odd beings who inhabit the planet.

> "Isn't it amazing," one such alien writes, "that these creatures have only two legs? It's incredible that they can move at all. And their hair actually grows. It doesn't stay at one pleasant length like ours."

An independent activity sheet, "These Earth People Are Too Much," is provided on page 198.

12. **Write a "Hello Human" letter.** Students pretend that they are animals who wish to communicate with humans. They can pretend to be pets, or less well known animals such as moles or bees.

If students wish to be serious, this activity can provide opportunities for research in which particular animals are studied. The animals can then write letters telling about themselves and their habits.

If students wish to be silly, they can use their imaginations and have fun with what animals might say to them. If a student has a cat, for example, would that cat complain about being fed only twice a day? In her letter, the cat might mention that she notices that her human eats all the time: chips, peanut butter sandwiches, glasses of milk. The unfairness of it is impossible to deny.

Use the independent activity sheet, "Hello Human," on page 199.

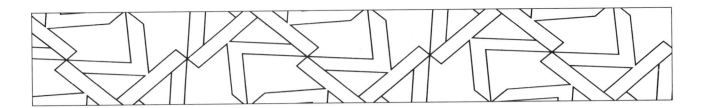

Something New

Write a letter to the Patent Office describing a new product you have created. For example, if you have invented a car that can find a parking space and can park itself, start your letter this way:

Dear Patent Officer,

    This vehicle will take the worry out of parking in the city.

Write your letter here:

_____ ,

_____

_____

_____

_____

_____

_____

_____

_____

_____

_____

_____

Name _____ **Date** _____

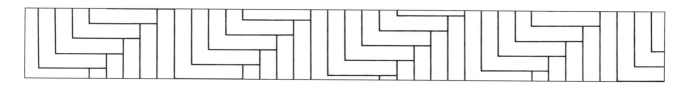

It's Horrible!

Imagine that you have spent good money on a product that completely disappoints you. Don't put up with it. Write a silly letter of complaint.

Perhaps, for example, you have just bought a new clock radio that has a mind of its own. You could start your letter with:

Dear Manufacturer,

This radio is beyond bad. It keeps turning its own volume up, and last night, it woke me up at 3 A.M., playing the National Anthem. I did not want to get up at 3 A.M.!

Write your letter here:

_____ ,

_____

_____

_____

_____

_____

_____

_____

_____

_____

Name _____ **Date** _____

Believe It!

Write a letter telling what you did not do this past weekend. For example, you probably didn't:

- Play in an NBA game and score 102 points.
- Stay at home and memorize the encyclopedia, A through M.
- Travel to Australia and pet a koala.

Write your letter here:

_____,

_____

_____

_____

_____

_____

_____

_____

_____

_____

_____

_____

Name _____ **Date** _____

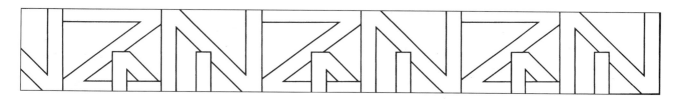

It's Very Strange Here

You have been transported to another planet or to a fantasy place on Earth. Write a letter that tells your friends what this new place is like. In this new place, for example, it's possible that:

- Pepperoni pizza grows on trees.
- Cats speak English.
- Tiny five-inch-tall people run around in plaid leotards.

Write your letter here:

_____ ,

_____

_____

_____

_____

_____

_____

_____

_____

_____

_____

_____

_____

Name _____ **Date** _____

These Earth People Are Too Much!

Pretend that you are an alien who is visiting Earth. Write a letter back to your friends telling them what this strange place and people are like. You could say, for example, that:

- The people are pleasant, but they all have such boring skin, not beautifully spotted like ours.
- Earthlings want to eat every day. It wastes so much time!

Write your letter here:

_____ ,

_____

_____

_____

_____

_____

_____

_____

_____

_____

_____

_____

Name _____ **Date** _____

Hello Human

Pretend that you are an animal who wishes to communicate with a human. Write a letter that expresses some of your thoughts and feelings. If you were a horse, for example, you could start with:

Dear Human,

    First of all, you are very heavy. How about going on a diet? Second, why don't I get to choose when we go for a ride?

Write your letter here:

_____ ,

_____

_____

_____

_____

_____

_____

_____

_____

_____

_____

                                                   _____

                                                   _____

Name _____   **Date** _____

USING THE NEWSPAPER

The newspaper is a valuable resource that you can use to encourage your students to write. It contains information on events that are happening now, and this is highly motivating to many students. Newspapers also have interesting sections like "Entertainment" and "Sports" that are particularly appealing.

Bring some newspapers to class. Read aloud one or two interesting articles, and then let students look through the papers to see what's there. You might list some of the sections on the chalkboard or on a large piece of paper. Allow students this time for exploration even if they are familiar with newspapers at home. In this way, you know they will have an overall view of what a paper contains.

If you live in an urban environment where the newspaper is very large, it is best to remove nonessential parts. This helps students feel that the paper is accessible to them—that it's not so big and bulky that it feels unmanageable.

An excellent way to proceed is to have students select a part of the newspaper they would like to write. Do they want to do a report on the weather, or write a front-page article on a local event? Would they like to write a movie review? Perhaps they could create the horoscope for the day, or write some classified ads.

One excellent resource you can use is the MAKE-YOUR-OWN-NEWSPAPERS!™ series from NEWSPOWER® (Harris Media Projects, 1988). For each newspaper, four 12″ × 15″ pages are provided. These pages are formatted with a newspaper structure, and space is given for students' writing. These newspapers are highly motivating because they are attractive and well organized. The prepared areas for students' writing will particularly help learners with spatial difficulties.

There are three levels: *My First Newspaper Series* (grades K–1), *The News Series* (grades 2–3), and *The Reporter* (grades 4 and up). The levels are geared more to age rather than to grade, and since the grade levels are not listed on the pages, you can freely choose the appropriate level for each student. You can write to NEWSPOWER, P.O. Box 203, Northfield, Massachusetts 01360, for a free catalogue which gives more information.

ACTIVITIES

The following favorite activities are spinoffs from sections of the newspaper. You can use them when your students need a change from the more traditional approach.

1. **Write descriptive sentences or paragraphs about interesting pictures from the newspaper.** Some examples of these pictures are:

   a. A young man with a Mohawk haircut carrying a pet rat on his head.

   b. A person on his mountain bike who is bungee jumping from a tower.

   c. A raccoon, who really understands the concept of central heating, curled up on top of a warm chimney.

   It helps some students if you first examine the picture and brainstorm key words that are inspired by it. Record these key words either on the chalkboard or on a large piece of paper. Students can then use them in their writing.

   This activity can be easily adapted for students who are working on word writing skills. Students can write descriptive words that come to mind as they look at the picture. They can also label sections of the photograph.

   Start a collection of interesting newspaper photographs for this activity.

2. **Write opinion sentences and paragraphs about interesting stories from the newspaper.** As with photographs, wonderful stories abound in the paper. For example, one told of a gorilla who rescued a child. After the boy had fallen onto the concrete floor of a gorilla exhibit, the animal picked up the toddler and brought him to a door where people could reach him. Another story told of a dog who pulled her paraplegic owner to safety from a burning van. A third told of an almost-one-thousand-pound sturgeon that was found dead in a lake in Washington. Talk about a fish story!

   Students enjoy hearing these stories, and they often have a lot to say about them. Invite them to do so in the form of sentences and paragraphs.

   Create a personal collection of these stories to develop a wide range of motivating topics.

3. **Create an ad for something you want to sell.** People advertise all kinds of products and services in the newspaper. With your students, examine several newspaper ads. Then, brainstorm what they would like to sell. Would they, for example, like to sell a new type of shoe? Perhaps parts of the top of this shoe are held on by Velcro, so that when it's warm outside, these portions can be taken off to create ventilation.

Would students prefer to advertise a service? They might want to start lawn mowing or child-care businesses.

These ads can be for real products, or for services that students would actually like to sell. They can also be imaginary. Some students particularly enjoy creating humorous advertisements. An independent activity sheet, "An Advertisement," is provided on page 205.

4. **Create a classified ad for an ideal job.** Many jobs are listed in the paper, but are they jobs that students would like? Encourage your students to dream about what they would like to do for a living. Then, examine some "Help Wanted" ads. Usually, these ads include information about educational and experience requirements. Ask your students to think about what their requirements are: What duties would they like to perform, and what would they like in a setting where they worked?

   This activity can be as basic or as complex as fits your students' levels and needs. An independent activity sheet, "Job Wanted," is provided on page 206.

5. **Write a Letter to the Editor that honors someone.** Often, this type of letter deals with issues. People express their opinions about things that are happening, especially in their local communities. A Letter to the Editor can also, however, honor a special person.

   Ask each student to think about a person whom he or she admires. This can be someone famous, a friend, or a member of the community. Help them to brainstorm several things they like about this person, including personal attributes and activities, and help them to start their letters.

   An independent activity sheet, "Someone Special," is provided on page 207.

6. **Write a "Dear Gertrude" letter.** Create a series of short letters, like the following:

   Dear Gertrude,

   I have been friends with Leon for two years. All of a sudden, he has stopped talking to me. What should I do?

   An unhappy friend

   Dear Gertrude,

   I have lots of homework every night, but I can't make myself do it. What should I do?

   A desperate student

Dear Gertrude,

I love my dog, but he has a really bad habit. Whenever I eat pizza, he jumps up on the table and grabs my pepperoni. And he's fast. I don't want to give up pizza, but it looks like it's the food or my dog. What should I do?

A confused dog owner

Dear Gertrude,

I have a serious problem. Sometimes, I am a clumsy oaf. Yesterday, I fell over my own shoelaces!

I'm a good athlete. I can run and jump with the best of them. But when I try to walk down the street: whoops, there I go again. Please help me.

Tired of falling

As you can see, the letters can be based in reality or in humor. You can create these letters to meet the levels and needs of your students. Once they are prepared, invite your students to become Gertrude and to answer them.

A "Dear Gertrude" independent activity sheet is provided on page 208.

7. **Write spectacular and not-necessarily-true newspaper headlines.** Examine some newspapers to see how the headlines call attention to particular articles. Record some favorite headlines on the chalkboard or on a large piece of paper.

   Invite your students to write some headlines of their own. They can make them as fabulous as they wish, as with the following:

   MAN BUILDS A LADDER AND CLIMBS TO THE MOON
   GIRL FINDS A LIVING BRONTOSAURUS
   500-POUND POTATO BAKED IN MAINE

   An independent activity sheet, "It Really Happened," is offered on page 209.

8. **Write a newspaper article for an event that has already occurred as if it were happening now.** Students can each select an event with which they are familiar. For example, if there was a major storm such as a hurricane in their area, they can write about that.

   This activity also offers good opportunities for research. Students can each select an event that they would like to learn about, and they can do research on this topic. They can check books or encyclopedias for information. One good series to look at is *Great Events, the Twentieth Century,* a Magill

Book from the editors of Salem Press (Salem Press, Inc., 1992). This series can be found in the reference room of many libraries.

9. **Write a newspaper article based on a fairy tale or fable.** Read some fairy tales and fables during read-aloud time. Then, ask your students to select a favorite one for which they would like to write an article. The article can either report what happened in the story or borrow the characters and create new incidents.

   Students have to remember, however, that newspaper reporters express no opinions. They must report only the facts: who is involved, what happened, and when it happened. Thus, an article on "Little Red Riding Hood" might start in the following way:

GIRL MEETS WOLF

   PUTNEY, VERMONT—Ms. R. Riding Hood reports that she was taking a basket of food to her sick grandmother, Ms. W. Walking Beret, early Wednesday afternoon, when she was approached by a wolf on Oak Street. Interviewed at her home on Wednesday evening, Ms. Hood reports that the wolf was initially pleasant and polite, and asked only for directions to the library.

   If students wish to do so, they can give an oral presentation of their articles. An independent activity sheet, "A Tale Retold," is offered on page 210.

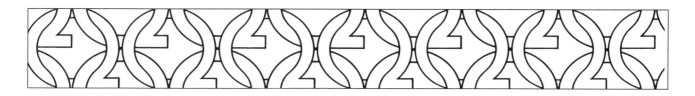

An Advertisement

Make an ad to sell a product. Do you want to sell a pencil that will correct misspelled words? Or a pair of sneakers that will let you jump four feet off the ground?

First, look at some newspapers and see how ads are presented. Then, design your ad here.

_____

_____

_____

_____

_____

_____

_____

_____

_____

_____

_____

_____

_____

_____

_____

_____

_____

_____

Name _____   **Date** _____

Job Wanted

Write an ad for a job that you would like. Remember to include information about the things you'd like to do, the kind of place where you'd like to work, and the amount of money you'd like to make. Your ad could start like this:

COMPUTER EXPERT

Wanted: A full-time job. The duties should include creating interactive computer games and . . .

Name _____   **Date** _____

Someone Special

Write a Letter to the Editor about a special person. Include information about why you like this person. Has this person done interesting things? Does she or he have personal characteristics that are admirable?

Such a letter could start like this:

Dear Friends,

I want to tell all of you about my Aunt Mabel. Lately, she hasn't traveled very far or done exciting things. She is, in fact, homebound because of illness. But my Aunt Mabel writes letters: to soldiers, to people in the hospital, to anyone whose life can be enriched by a letter.

_____ ,

_____

_____

_____

_____

_____

_____

_____

_____

_____

_____

                                        _____

                                        _____

Name _____   **Date** _____

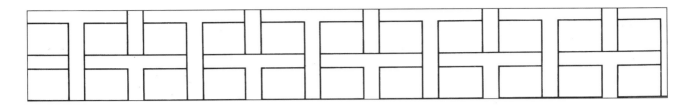

Dear Gertrude

Pretend that you are Gertrude and answer the following letter.

Dear Gertrude,

    I bought a used car yesterday, and I loved it for the first ten miles. But then, when I stopped for a red light, the hood fell off. Really. The hood slipped off the front of the car onto the road.

    The place where I bought it says I don't need a hood. They say I can cover the front of the car with plastic wrap. What should I do?

A disappointed car owner

Dear Disappointed,

_____

_____

_____

_____

_____

_____

_____

_____

_____

_____

_____

Gertrude

© 1997 by Cynthia M. Stowe

Name _____ **Date** _____

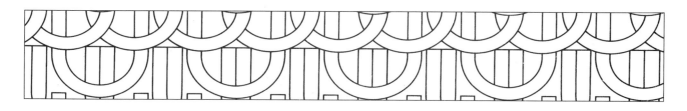

It Really Happened

Write some newspaper headlines. Remember, they don't necessarily have to be true, like the following:

SALMON SAVES DROWNING MAN!

WOMAN TIPTOES ACROSS THE UNITED STATES!

UNDERSEA ANCIENT CASTLE DISCOVERED!

Name _____   **Date** _____

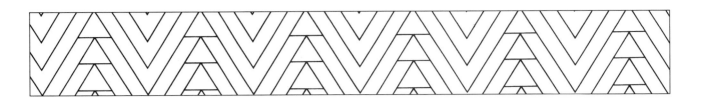

A Tale Retold

Pretend that you are a newspaper reporter who lives in the same town as the three little pigs. You have been assigned to cover the story of one of their less well known encounters with the wolf. You could start your article in this way:

A WOLF GONE ASTRAY

BACONVILLE, Ohio—Mr. I. M. Pig confided to this reporter that he and his two brothers no longer feel safe in their own home because of a recent incident with their neighbor, Mr. A. Wolf. The three pigs were mowing the lawn and doing yard work when . . .

Name _____   **Date** _____

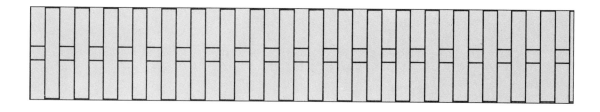

INTEGRATING WRITING WITH REAL LIFE AND THE REST OF THE CURRICULUM

You can encourage your students to see writing as a necessary life skill by demonstrating many situations where the ability to write is needed. This can be highly motivating to students, and can encourage them to work hard at this skill.

Similarly, writing cannot really be separated from the rest of the curriculum. All subjects involve some form of writing—from writing numbers in mathematics to writing essays in English. It's beneficial to a writing program—and most probably to other subjects as well—if you integrate the curriculum as much as is possible.

ACTIVITIES

In the following, each activity is labeled as to its major area of integration. Concerning the connection of writing with subject matter, the activities listed have proven to be effective. They are offered as examples of the many ways which integration can occur. No examples for Reading or English will be presented, since the "Literature Connection" chapter contains many of them.

1. **Real Life: Fill out forms.** Some common forms are:
   - Signature cards for opening a bank account
   - Savings Deposit slips for banks
   - Savings Withdrawal slips for banks
   - Credit card applications
   - Loan applications
   - Library card applications

   People in banks and other institutions are usually very gracious about providing samples of these forms, and students are motivated to learn how to complete them when they have the official versions. For students who, because of spatial issues, need some practice before completing actual forms, simplified versions of a Savings Deposit slip and a Savings Withdrawal slip are provided on page 216.

Speak with people in your local community about teaching your students to fill out forms correctly. Business people can sometimes offer great help. As an example, a banking program called SAVING MAKES "CENTS" is coordinated between the Treasurer of the Commonwealth of Massachusetts, some schools, and individual banks such as the Greenfield Cooperative Bank in Greenfield, Massachusetts. In 1995, 60,000 students were educated about banking, and there was certainly some writing involved.

You may discover good programs in your area. Even if you don't, you most probably will find people who are willing to help—by providing materials or even coming to school to speak. All this exposure to real-life forms will help your students begin to feel comfortable with them.

2. **Real Life: Write checks.** Checking accounts are important tools in modern life, and students profit from learning about them. As with the other forms, you can speak with bankers in your area to see if they can help with this work. Some banks provide blank, unofficial checks for educational use.

You can also ask families and friends if they have unused checks from closed accounts. By placing a label over the important identifying information, you can make it clear that the checks are being used for practice purposes only.

Simplified check forms are also provided on page 217. If you can't find other checks, or your students need to begin with a less complex version, you can use these forms.

Students profit greatly from practicing writing their names and dates and the amounts of money being transacted. If possible, it's also good to provide some type of bank register with which students can keep track of money spent.

An interesting checking account program is carried out at Eagle Mountain School in Greenfield, Massachusetts. Every student receives a "paycheck" of Eagle Mountain dollars (pretend currency, of course) at the end of each month. They can earn additional dollars by completing extra work or by winning games.

This money is deposited into checking accounts. Various catalogues such as for clothing, sports equipment, and computer software are provided. Students can then order things from these catalogues (more good writing practice).

Even though nothing but pretend money and possessions are involved, this checking account system has proven to be highly motivating. Students have a lot of fun with it, and they gain valuable skills.

3. **Real Life: Fill out job applications.** As with other forms, it's best to go to two or three businesses and tell them what you are doing. Most people are happy to give you a few forms with which your students can practice.

   Even though filling out applications is highly motivating, especially to older students, some of the applications can appear very complex and overwhelming. For this reason, it's best to start with the simplified form on page 218. Once students feel comfortable with this, they will more easily move into real-life versions.

4. **Real Life: Leave messages for peers and teachers in a message area in the classroom.** The creation of a message area requires effort. If money for school supplies is available, it can be purchased. Some educational supply companies sell a large cardboard unit that is divided into individual sections.

   If you can't afford to purchase such a message center, you can make one out of a large box, or use a series of envelopes, one large envelope for each student.

   It's important to model leaving messages. You can leave notes to students congratulating them for work well done, or you can ask them such questions as "Did you watch the football game on TV last night?" They are expected to answer you by placing a note in your "post office box." You can also leave such reminders as "Please bring your book about Michael Jordan to school tomorrow." Once students become familiar with using the message center, they enjoy using it for communication.

5. **Real Life: Write shopping lists.** This activity is unusual in that it is something that students do at home. Often, parents ask, "What can I do? How can I help my child?" Offer keeping a shopping list as a suggestion.

   A piece of lined paper is placed on the refrigerator with a magnet. Every time a food supply is running short, it is recorded on the shopping list. At first, parents model recording the needed supplies, and when appropriate, ask a child to do so. Then, the shopping list becomes a community project: Whoever notices that a food is needed records the information.

   This seems like a very simple activity. If done consistently and with positive feedback, however, it can help students recognize that writing is an important life skill.

6. **Mathematics: Write math word problems.** This idea was discovered in *Really Writing! Ready-to-Use Writing Process Activities for the Elementary Grades* by Cheryl Sunflower (The Center for Applied Research in Education,

1994). Gratitude is expressed to the author, since this idea has proven to be very effective with students with special needs.

Students at all levels of writing and math skill can write these problems. For students at word writing levels, provide a framework like the following:

> Tony had _____ pieces of bubblegum, and he bought more. How many pieces of bubblegum did Tony have altogether?
>
> Answer _____

Students complete the problem with written numbers.

These problems can be written at all levels of complexity. Students sometimes enjoy writing a group of problems and then combining them into a booklet with which other students can work.

7. **Science: Make a science record notebook.** Many scientists have kept these notebooks. Thomas Edison, for example, kept records of experiments, recording both diagrams and text.

   This activity can be effective with all levels of students, but it is particularly potent with beginning writers, especially writers who are unmotivated and who do not yet see writing as having any meaning in their lives. For example, one young student who actively resisted all forms of writing, probably because of failure experiences in the past, *was* very interested in constructing things. It was agreed that he could spend some time building a cardboard "home" for a small stuffed animal in the classroom if, in return, he would record the day's date and write down what he had done. In the beginning, it seemed that keeping this science record was, for this student, merely a way to earn free time to do what he really wanted to do. Each daily record was one sentence like, "I built a roof."

   As time went on, however, the student began to like looking back on what he had written. Even though the entries were short, they did tell a story—a real-life story that he had created. His resistance to writing entries for the journal decreased dramatically, and he began to willingly participate in other forms of writing as well.

8. **Science: Write a science shape poem.** The idea for a shape poem is also from *Really Writing!* and is discussed fully on pages 145–146 in the "Poetry" chapter of this book.

   For this poem, students draw a simple picture of an object associated with something they are studying in science. Are they studying snails, for example, or turtles? Are they learning about trees, or the various types of root systems for plants? Are they studying the wonders of clouds?

Students brainstorm facts and impressions they have gained. Then, they write their favorites on the lines of their drawings.

In a variation of this poem, students fill in their shapes, as opposed to outlining them with writing. Some shapes, such as that of a tornado, make particularly interesting poems when done in this way.

9. **Social Studies: Make postcards from other countries.** This simple activity is fun for most students. They pretend that they are visiting a country, which they are coincidentally studying in class.

   You will need some 4″ × 6″ lined index cards. On the unlined side, each student draws a picture depicting a scene from the country. On the lined side, she writes the address of the person who will receive the card, and a short message. It's best if she can include some information that is relevant to the area she is visiting. For example, if she is visiting Australia, she could say, "The temperature is hot here in December. But, then again, it's summer in this part of the world."

   If stamps are available, students enjoy actually mailing their cards. If not, they can "mail" them to students at school.

10. **Social Studies: Record oral history.** The opportunities for writing are limitless. At the most advanced level, students can create books, like the series of *Foxfire* books published by Anchor Books, Anchor Press/Doubleday. For these books, students interviewed older people about earlier times in the Appalachian Mountains.

    Students can also, however, record oral history in many other ways. If they are working at word writing skills, they can write lists of interesting information, like the following:

    - ways that people made a living

    - things that people did for recreation

    - things we have in modern life that people did not know about then

    - customs for a particular day of the week, such as Saturday or Sunday

    - what would happen on a typical day at work or school

    Students can write sentences about what they have learned from talking with older people. They can also write opinion paragraphs about what they have discovered.

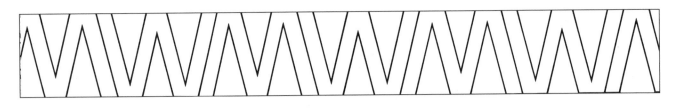

Banking Forms

DEPOSIT SLIP

	Dollars	Cents
Cash		
Checks		
Total		

Name _____

Address _____

_____

Date _____

Account # _____

WITHDRAWAL SLIP

Date _____

Pay to me or _____

Amount of money _____
(write in words)

Signature _____

Address _____

Account # _____

Name _____   **Date** _____

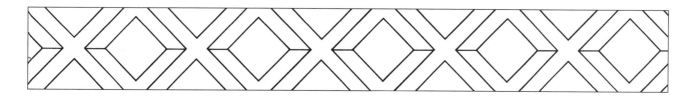

Checks

A CHECK

Date _____ 20 ___

Pay to the
Order of _____ $ _____

_____ Dollars
(write in words)

_____
Signature

A CHECK

Date _____ 20 ___

Pay to the
Order of _____ $ _____

_____ Dollars
(write in words)

_____
Signature

Name _____ **Date** _____

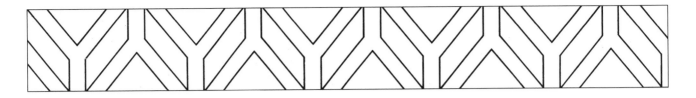

A Job Application

Date _____

Name _____

Social Security Number _____

Address _____

Telephone Number _____

Are you legally available
for work in the U.S.A.?   Yes _____   No _____

Name of your school _____

School address _____

Last grade completed _____

Employment Record

Company name _____

Address _____

Your position and duties _____

_____

Why did you leave? _____

_____

References

Name _____   Phone _____

Name _____   Phone _____

What kind of job are you seeking? _____ Full or Part Time _____

Name _____   **Date** _____

GIMMICKS AND GAGS

The activities in this section are diverse, and utilize many modalities. They are placed together because they are highly motivational. Students enjoy these activities and relax while doing them.

If it appears that your students are tired or feeling some frustration as they are working on their writing, offer an activity from this section—as a help in pacing the program. Students will continue to develop their writing skills, but it won't feel like "work" to them. Even if your students are functioning at a higher level, such as writing research reports or essays, they can still profit from the rest and the practice that these activities provide.

The activities in this section are divided into the following categories:

1. Games that develop auditory and verbal skills
2. Activities and games for the development of word writing
3. Activities and games for the development of sentence writing
4. Activities for the development of paragraph writing

ACTIVITIES

Games That Develop Auditory and Verbal Skills

1. **Listen carefully to sounds.** Collect a group of objects that, when struck or dropped or otherwise manipulated, will make a sound. Musical instruments like a recorder or a drum are very effective for this purpose. Show your students the objects and tell them that you are going to make some sounds with them. Their job is to listen carefully.

   Ask your students to close their eyes. Then, make a sound with one of the objects. Next, ask your students to open their eyes and to tell you about the sound they have just heard. Repeat this activity for as long as your students are interested and motivated.

2. **Listen carefully to the environment.** Tell your students that you are going to ask them to close their eyes and to sit quietly and listen for two minutes.

219

Once the time is up, you will ask them to open their eyes and to talk about the sounds they have heard.

If you wish, you may write down the different sounds on a large piece of paper or on the chalkboard.

3. **Play the "How Does It End?" game.** This activity can be presented once students are familiar with the ending punctuation marks of periods and question marks. This activity specifically encourages students to listen carefully and in a discriminating manner to spoken language. They begin to hear the "music" of the spoken word. This, in turn, helps them to recognize complete sentences in their writing.

Give each student two index cards—one with a period written on it, the other with a question mark. Say a series of sentences, some of which are statements and others, questions. Each student is asked to listen carefully to each sentence and to hold up the correct ending punctuation mark.

Activities and Games for the Development of Word Writing

1. **Play the "Draw the Music" game.** For this activity, you will need a tape recorder and a selection of four different types of music—for example, classical, country, rock and roll, and jazz. Crayons, felt pens, or colored pencils are also needed.

Get large pieces of paper and ask your students to fold them lengthwise and crosswise so that four equal sections are created. Play one of the tapes. Ask your students to draw a picture of how the music makes them feel in one of their sections of paper. Ask them also to write words or phrases that are inspired by the music.

Then, play the next tape, and so on. When all four tapes have been played, ask students to share their impressions.

2. **Draw words.** Students make visual representations of what words mean, for example:

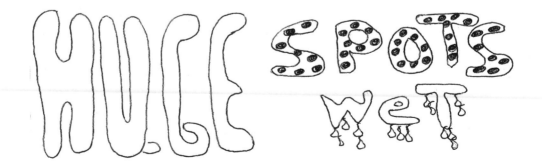

Students enjoy thinking of many different words to "draw." They often like to collect their drawings into notebooks or bound books. Sometimes a group of students will enjoy making a cooperative book.

This activity is particularly helpful with students who have positive feelings about art, but who have experienced a great deal of frustration with writing. This activity helps them begin to relax around the written word.

3. **Make word design pictures.** First, students get some drawing paper and felt pens or colored pencils. Next, they each select one word they wish to use for their design.

   Then, in very large letters, they each repeatedly "write" their word on the paper. It is often effective to write the word diagonally between the four corners and then to border the paper with the word. If they wish, students can color their completed word design pictures.

4. **Make tin can labels.** This activity requires preparation. You must first clean some tin cans and carefully peel off the paper labels. Create patterns from the labels, which students will then trace on regular paper and cut out.

   Some students like to make labels for typical foods. Others like to use less usual foods or even invent some of their own.

   This activity can be adapted to meet the level and needs of your students. For some, it will be a learning experience to write the brand name and name of the food on the label. Others will enjoy the challenge of listing ingredients and nutrition facts and, perhaps, even inventing a recipe. Once the writing is done, students decorate their labels and attach them to tin cans. An independent activity sheet, "A Tin Can Label," is provided on page 225.

5. **Make an architectural drawing or a map.** Architectural drawings can represent any kind of structure such as a room, a house, or an office building. A map can represent a city, state, or country, or a smaller area such as a school yard or a park. These subjects can be real or imaginary. Two independent activity sheets, "An Architectural Drawing," and "A Map" are provided on pages 226 and 227.

6. **Make and play a sentence rummy game.** Ask students to write words, one per card, on 3″ × 5″ index cards. Encourage them to include nouns and verbs if they have already been introduced to these concepts. Then, make some cards yourself. The following are good ones to include:

   • (Nouns) boy, girl, dog, elephant, airplane, bus, pizza, book, Alaska, baseball

   • (Verbs) got, ran, saw, fell, sat, ate, flew, helped, played, looked

   • (Pronouns) he, his, him, she, her, they, their, them, it

   • (Articles, Conjunctions, and Prepositions) the, a, an, and, to, on, of, with, for, at

Place twenty blank cards in the card deck. These are free cards, for which players can make up any word they wish.

Players each get six cards to start. In turn, they take one card from the top of the card deck. Players make sentences by placing appropriate words on the table. During the game, a player may continue to make new sentences or add to an existing sentence. At the end of the game, the player who has placed down the most cards is the winner.

7. **Write a menu.** Writing menus is a lot of fun. These menus can be for a meal that a student is planning to make, or it can be for an imaginary meal. Some students enjoy using humor, and they create outrageous foods and interesting combinations of foods. An independent activity sheet, "A Menu," is provided on page 228.

Activities and Games for the Development of Sentence Writing

1. **Make and play your own trivia game.** In this game, students make a deck of cards by writing a factual question on one side of a 3″ × 5″ index card, and the answer in a complete sentence on the other side of the card. A game board is then made on which players move a certain number of steps, determined by the roll of a die. Players START at a given place and proceed toward an END.

   The first player starts the game by rolling the die and then moving her piece (a button or a small object) that number of places. She then picks a card from the deck. If she can correctly answer the question, she stays where she is. If not, she returns to her original position until her next turn. The winner is the first person to reach the END.

2. **Write directions.** Directions can be written for such diverse topics as:
   - how to comb my hair
   - how to eat a chocolate chip cookie (make sure students are not allergic to any ingredients)
   - how to walk across the street

   Students number their papers and write one sentence for each instruction. Then, they follow their own directions. An independent activity sheet, "Write Directions," is provided on page 229.

   You can vary this activity in many ways. One such variation is to make it a competitive game. Tell students that the person who writes the highest number of instructions for a given task will be declared the winner. This encourages very detailed directions . . . and lots of sentences.

3. **Write riddles.** These can be simple, such as "This thing is red. You can eat it. What is it?" (answer: an apple)

     The riddles can also be more complex, where students first select a noun (the answer). Next, they write a series of characteristics. Last, they make up a riddle that contains two diverse and seemingly contradictory characteristics. An example of the latter follows:

   • The Answer: eyes

   • Characteristics: can be different colors, work as a team, have lids and lashes, are set apart in the face, let people and animals see

   • The Riddle: They never meet but do their best work together. Who are they?

4. **Write and draw the literal "meanings" of clichés.** Students first write down as many clichés as they can think of—for example:

   • She's driving me up the wall.

   • This car is a lemon.

   • Money burns a hole in his pocket.

     Students can consult with others to collect as many clichés as they can. They then select a few that will make humorous drawings. Students write one cliché per page and make a drawing of its literal meaning. Sometimes, students enjoy making a book of their drawings.

5. **Play the "Draw a Monster" game.** Form teams of two people each. Tell your students that they will be drawing an interesting monster. (You can also have them draw a race car, or some other appropriate object.) They must hide their drawings from their partners, because once they are done, each partner is going to try to duplicate the other's drawing. Written directions will be provided by the original creator.

     It is best to provide a model for students to help them get started writing directions. For instance, you can write on the chalkboard or on a large piece of paper:

     My monster is _____ inches high and _____ inches wide.

     His head is _____ (a circle or a square or . . .)

     The independent activity sheet, "Draw a Monster," on page 230, gives more information on this activity.

Activities for the Development of Paragraph Writing

1. **Write television commercials.** Students will particularly enjoy this activity because, to prepare for it, they have to watch TV. Ask them to carefully watch several commercials. Next, they must decide on the product they will

be selling. Then, they should write out the setting and the dialogue for the commercial. This is an example:

> A woman is sitting on the floor in front of her washing machine. She is holding a stained shirt. She is crying.
> "Oh no," she says. "Henry needs this for his performance tonight. What am I going to do?"

If students wish, they can accompany their narratives with art. They can also produce their commercials for the class to see. An independent activity sheet, "A TV Commercial," is provided on page 231.

2. **Conduct a ridiculous interview.** Students each write a series of questions to ask selected people. The interesting aspect of this activity, however, is that the people are not exactly available to answer them. That is because they are either historical or imaginary figures, such as Julius Caesar or a "person" who lives on the moon.

Students imagine that they are speaking with these people. They ask their questions and make notes about the answers. Then, they write out the information gained in a series of statements. If you wish, you can teach the technique of putting each statement on a separate piece of small paper, which can then be arranged into logical content groups.

Students organize their information into paragraphs and, if they wish to do so, present their "interviews" to their peers. An independent activity sheet, "A Ridiculous Interview," is provided on page 232.

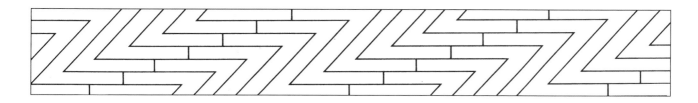

A Tin Can Label

Get an empty tin can from home or from the school cafeteria. Clean it and carefully peel off the paper label. Look at the label carefully to see the information it contains. Then, trace the label on a clean sheet of drawing paper and cut it out.

You are now ready to make your own tin can label, but don't feel that your food has to be real—like green beans or corn. If you wish, you can invent a "new" food.

For example, how about Zurk? Zurk is a fruit that is grown in special greenhouses in Texas. It has no fat, no cholesterol, and no sodium. It is so healthy that one bite gives you all the vitamins, minerals, and fiber you need for one week.

Make notes about your food here.

_____

_____

_____

_____

_____

_____

_____

_____

_____

_____

_____

_____

_____

_____

Name _____ **Date** _____

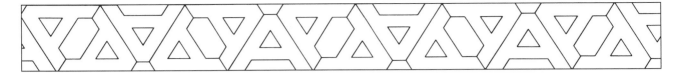

An Architectural Drawing

Imagine that you are a very tiny person who is living in the stump of an old redwood tree. You are energetic. You have tools. You have created a comfortable home with many rooms. You even have a solar-heated hot tub on your roof!

Make an architectural drawing of your home. Label all the rooms and any special luxuries.

Name _____   **Date** _____

A Map

Imagine a perfect place to live. Will it be in the forest or in a big city? Will you have a pond, a park, churches, schools, and a mall?

　　Make some notes here about some things you would like in your perfect place.

_____

_____

_____

_____

_____

_____

_____

_____

_____

_____

_____

_____

_____

_____

　　Now pretend that you are a bird looking down on your place. On a separate sheet of unlined paper, draw a map. Label all the important parts, such as roads, buildings, and rivers.

Name _____ **Date** _____

A Menu

Pretend that you are having company for supper—visitors from Mars! You have been told that these Martians are bored with regular food, and that they want to eat something interesting.

Your mission: Plan an exciting menu.

If you fail: All Mars™ candy bars will be eliminated from the Earth.

Your menu might start with these snacks before the main meal:

- Spinach roll-ups (spinach leaves filled with peanut butter)
- Mushroom squares (mushrooms frozen in little cubes of ice).

Write down your menu here.

_____

_____

_____

_____

_____

_____

_____

_____

_____

_____

_____

Name _____ **Date** _____

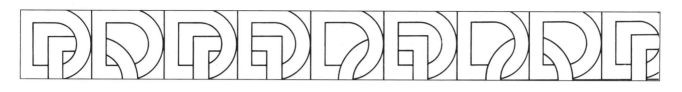

Write Directions

You probably think that it is easy to bounce a ball. But what if you were trying to teach someone who had never seen or felt one?

Find a friend who wishes to play a game. You both will write directions for how to bounce a ball. Then, each of you will follow the other's directions. You could start like this:

1. Place your hand on the ball.
2. Close your fingers around the ball.

Write your directions here. (Other things that you can write directions for are: how to play with a yo-yo, how to jump rope, how to pet a friendly cat, how to peel a potato, how to make a "snake" out of clay, how to staple two pieces of paper together, and how to put a stamp on an envelope.)

_____

_____

_____

_____

_____

_____

_____

_____

_____

_____

_____

Name _____ **Date** _____

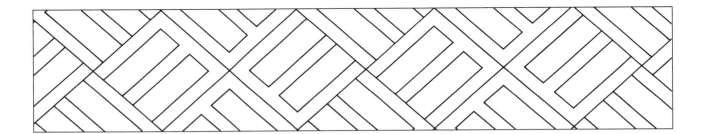

Draw a Monster

Find a friend who wants to play the DRAW A MONSTER game. Without letting each other see what you are doing, both of you draw a monster. Then, write directions for how to duplicate your creation.

This is a good way to start:

My monster is _____ inches tall and _____ inches wide.

She has a head that looks like a _____ .

Her body is the shape of a _____ .

My monster has _____ arms.

Each arm is _____ inches long and _____ inches wide.

Once the directions are written, each of you draws the other person's monster. See how close you can get to the original.

Write your directions here.

_____

_____

_____

_____

_____

_____

_____

_____

_____

_____

Name _____ **Date** _____

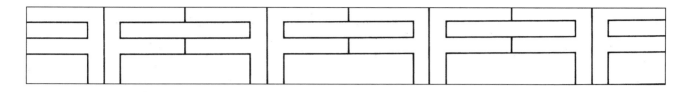

A TV Commercial

Write a TV commercial. First, watch a few commercials to see how they are organized. Then, decide on the product you will be selling. This can be real or imaginary. Write down your product here.

_____

Next, decide on the setting. Will your commercial take place in a home, in a store, on a hillside, or in some other setting? Write down your setting here.

_____

Last, think about the dialogue. Will one person talk to the camera, or will two people talk to each other? For example:

(Two girls are sitting at the roadside next to bicycles with flat tires.)

"Too bad we didn't see that glass," Helen said.

"It's okay," Liu said. "Remember, we have those terrific tires that fix themselves. They should start working soon."

Start your dialogue here:

_____

_____

_____

_____

_____

_____

_____

_____

Name _____   **Date** _____

A Ridiculous Interview

It's enjoyable to interview people because you find out unexpected things. But what if the "person" you are interviewing is not exactly alive? You would then be able to create the questions . . . and the answers.

For example, what if you were interviewing someone like Batman? Your interview might start like this:

Interviewer: "Why did you start fighting crime?"

Batman: "I hate crooks."

Interviewer: "What kind of crooks do you hate the most?"

Batman: "Ones who cheat and steal, but mostly I hate crooks who have dandruff."

Interviewer: "What do you like?"

Batman: "Truth, justice, and the American way."

Interviewer: "What else?"

Batman: "Ice cream and pizza pie with anchovies."

Start your interview here.

_____

_____

_____

_____

_____

_____

_____

_____

_____

Name _____ **Date** _____

APPENDIX A

The following ideas for writing lists are arranged approximately in order of level of difficulty, from tangible to more abstract, and from word writing to phrase, and then sentence writing.

All students benefit from writing lists. For beginning students, it provides a task that can be accomplished independently, because as much structure as is needed can be provided to ensure success. While working on these enjoyable and easy lists, students can begin to overcome any fear or insecurity they may have of writing.

More advanced students also have an enjoyable experience with this activity. They gain valuable practice writing words and sentences.

Academically, writing lists supports the development of word retrieval, logical thinking, and critical thinking skills. Students focus on thinking of details that fit in specific categories. Thus, they gain practice in thinking of what to write about. They get so used to putting their thoughts on paper that they feel freer to do so with other writing tasks.

Choose list topics that are easy for your students, and provide as much structure and help as is needed for them to be successful. For example, if they need to see specific objects in order to name them, as in the "things on the table" idea, repeat this activity as many times as is necessary. If the list topic for the day is "things you can put on your feet," bring in a few samples of some shoes, slippers, and socks. Surprise everyone with an unusual object, such as a Band-Aid, which can go on a foot. If the list topic is "things associated with baseball," first read a poem about baseball and use the images present within it to start the list.

With students functioning at all levels, it is good to start with safe, easy list ideas. Once students are comfortable with this activity, more challenging ones can be introduced.

The topics listed below are only a few of the unlimited possibilities. Your students will enjoy adding many more great ideas of their own.

LIST IDEAS

- things on the table (Place objects on the table which your students can record.)

- things in this room
- things bigger than . . . (This can be any object placed on the table. Sometimes, students enjoy being the "bigger than"—for example: "Write a list of things that are bigger than Willi.")
- things smaller than . . . (As with the "bigger than" list, the stimulus can be an object or an animal or a person.)
- things that can fit in a particular box (The box, or any other container, is placed on the table.)
- things that are red (All other colors can also be used.)
- things that are depicted in a presented picture (This picture can be a page in a picture book or any other stimulus picture.)
- food
- vegetables
- fruit
- toppings for pizza
- ice cream flavors
- food you can put on top of a pancake
- colors
- flowers
- clothing
- kinds of hats
- kinds of shoes
- kinds of shirts
- things you can put on your hands
- things you can put on your feet
- animals
- animals with wings
- animals without wings
- wild animals
- pets
- jungle animals
- kinds of cats
- birds
- amphibians
- reptiles
- mammals
- fish
- insects
- things found in a house or apartment
- things found in a garage
- things found in a barn

- things found in a kitchen (and other rooms in a home)
- things found in a jungle
- things found in a city park
- things found in the forest
✓ • things found on a ship
- things found in a garden
- things found on a farm
- names of people
- names of animals (dogs, cats, horses, etc.)
- kinds of homes
- forms of transportation
✓ • tools
- prizes
- things that fly
- things that swim
- things that can float
- things that can jump
- things that can move fast
- things that grow
- ways of moving
- favorite restaurants
- farm equipment
- kinds of cars and trucks
- kinds of furniture
- bodies of water
- street names
- three-letter words (or other kinds of words, such as words with specified numbers of syllables or words that begin with a selected letter)
- things associated with a particular season of the year
- things that can be baked
- things that melt
✓ • kinds of stores
- things made out of metal
- things made out of glass
- things made out of wood
✓ • things made out of paper
- things made out of bricks
- things associated with sports (or any particular sport such as basketball)
✓ • names of baseball teams (and other types of teams)
- kinds of jobs
- sharp things

- things that have wheels
- things that have motors
- things that use oil
- book titles
- song titles
- movie titles
- uses for a box
- uses for a pencil
- things that are related to music
- things that are related to the movies
- things you would like to take on a three-day camping trip
- things you would like to find in a box that you discover behind an abandoned building
- things you can do on a rainy day (or a snowy day, or a sunny day)
- ways of getting across the street without letting your feet touch the ground
- things that make you happy
- the similarities that all people share
- ways to play
- natural mysteries in the world (such as the Bermuda Triangle)
- wishes (personal wishes or wishes for others)
- things you are going to do later today
- things you did yesterday
- excuses for not doing homework
- ways to avoid working
- ways to annoy a teacher (or a parent, or a friend)
- things that are easy for you to accomplish
- reasons not to smoke cigarettes
- reasons not to experiment with drugs
- things you would do with a million dollars
- what you would do if you were in charge of the world

APPENDIX B

Written language does differ from conversational English, and for this reason, it is important for beginning writers to listen to the written word. Therefore, reading aloud is an important part of the *Let's Write!* program. Usually, this occurs for approximately ten minutes at the end of class. Sometimes, however, especially for students with attention or behavior issues, it helps also to start class with a short read-aloud selection.

Jim Trelease thoroughly discusses the benefits of reading aloud to students in *The Read-Aloud Handbook*, revised and updated, including a giant treasure of great read-aloud books, 4th ed. (Penguin Books, 1995). Other good resources for finding good read-aloud material are:

Books Children Love, a Guide to the Best Children's Literature by Elizabeth Wilson, foreword by Susan Schaeffer Macaulay (Crossway Books, 1987).
The New York Times Parent's Guide to the Best Books for Children by Eden Ross Lipson, Children's Book Editor of the *New York Times* (Times Books, 1988).
Books to Build On, a Grade-by-Grade Resource Guide for Parents and Teachers, edited by John Holdren and E. D. Hirsch, Jr., (Delta, 1996).
Reading Rainbow Guide to Children's Books, the 101 Best Titles by Twila Liggett, Ph.D., and Cynthia Mayer Benfield, with an introduction by LeVar Burton (A Citadel Press Book, Published by Carol Publishing Group, 1994, 1996).

You can also find good books by attending conferences on children's literature, speaking with other people, and just browsing in your local library. In addition to stories, look at other kinds of books such as:

- joke and riddle books
- nonfiction books
- poetry books (some good poetry selections are cited in the "Poetry" chapter of this book)
- folk tales
- biographies

The possibilities are endless, and the more you search and read, the more you will find. The basic rule for selecting books is this: Read books that you and your students enjoy. Read-aloud time should be fun and relaxing. This will optimize its effectiveness.

The following are some favorite books.

PICTURE BOOKS

Ashanti To Zulu by Margaret Musgrove, illustrated by Leo and Diane Dillon (Dial Press, 1976).

Crow Boy, written and illustrated by Taro Yashima (Viking, 1955).

Lyle, Lyle, Crocodile, written and illustrated by Bernard Waber, (Houghton Mifflin, 1965).

Miss Nelson Is Missing! by Harry Allard, illustrated by James Marshall (Houghton Mifflin, 1977).

Pinkerton, Behave, written and illustrated by Steven Kellogg (Dial, 1979).

Strega Nona, written and illustrated by Tomie dePaola (Prentice Hall, 1975).

The Amazing Bone, written and illustrated by William Steig (Farrar, Straus and Giroux, 1976).

The Empty Pot by Demi (Henry Holt, 1990).

The Red Comb by Fernando Picó, illustrated by Maria Antonia Odonez, adapted and published in English by BridgeWater Books, 1994, copyright by Ediciones Huracan of Puerto Rico in 1991 and Ediciones Ekare of Venezuela in 1991).

The Stonecutter: A Japanese Folktale, written and illustrated by Gerald McDermott (Viking, 1975).

Thy Friend Obadiah, written and illustrated by Brinton Turkle (Viking, 1969).

CHAPTER BOOKS AND NOVELS

A Nose For Trouble by Nancy Hope Wilson, illustrated by Doron Ben-Ami (Avon, 1994).

Ben And Me, written and illustrated by Robert Lawson (Little, Brown, 1939).

Beware The Mare by Jesse Haas, pictures by Martha Haas (Greenwillow Books, 1993).

Bunnicula: A Rabbit Tale of Mystery by Deborah and James Howe, illustrated by Alan Daniel (Atheneum, 1979).

Call It Courage by Armstrong Sperry (Macmillan, 1968).

Charlotte's Web by E. B. White, illustrated by Garth Williams (Harper, 1952).

Did You Carry the Flag Today, Charley? by Rebecca Caudill, illustrated by Nancy Grossman (Holt, Rinehart and Winston, 1966).

From the Mixed-Up Files of Mrs. Basil E. Frankweiler, written and illustrated by E. L. Konigsburg (Atheneum, 1967).

How To Eat Fried Worms by Thomas Rockwell, illustrated by Emily McCully (Watts, 1973).

Letters From Rifka by Karen Hesse (Henry Holt, 1992).

Morning Girl by Michael Dorris (Hyperion, 1992).

One Fat Summer by Robert Lipsyte (Harper & Row, 1977).

Rabbit Hill by Robert Lawson (Viking, 1944).

Sing Down The Moon by Scott O'Dell (Houghton Mifflin, 1970).

Slake's Limbo by Felice Holman (Scribner, 1974).

Snow Treasure by Marie McSwigan, illustrated by André LaBlanc (Scholastic, 1996).

The Best Christmas Pageant Ever by Barbara Robinson, illustrated by Judith Gwyn Brown (Harper & Row, 1972).

The Contender by Robert Lipsyte (Harper & Row, 1967).

The Diary of a Young Girl by Anne Frank (Pocket Books, 1958).

The Hoboken Chicken Emergency by D. Manus Pinkwater (Aladdin Paperbacks, 1977).

The Lion, the Witch and the Wardrobe by C. S. Lewis (Macmillan, 1983).

The Stories Julian Tells by Ann Cameron, illustrated by Ann Strugnell (Pantheon, 1981).

The Summer Of My German Soldier by Bette Greene (Dial, 1973).

ANTHOLOGIES AND BOOKS OF SHORT STORIES

Fables by Arnold Lobel (Harper & Row, 1980).

Houseful Of Laughter by Bennett Cerf (Random House, 1963).

The Random House Book of Humor, selected by Pamela Pollack, illustrated by Paul Zelinsky (Random House, 1988).

Tongues of Jade by Laurence Yep, illustrated by David Wiesner (HarperCollins, 1991).

Thirty-Three Multicultural Tales to Tell by Pleasant DeSpain, illustrated by Joe Shlichta (August House, 1993).

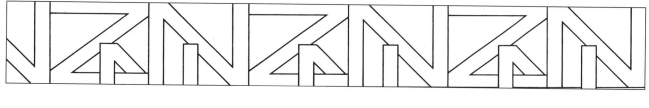

NOTES

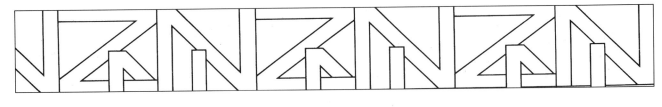

NOTES

NOTES

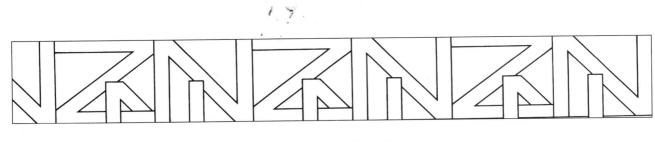

NOTES

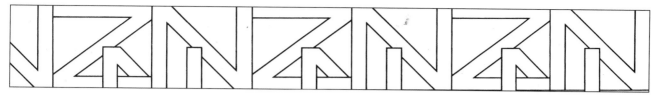

NOTES

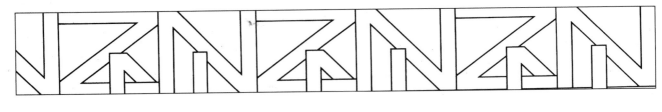

NOTES